Playtime Pottery
& Porcelain

From Europe & Asia

Lorraine Punchard

77 Lower Valley Road, Atglen, PA 19310

This book is dedicated to my family,
My Husband Richard V. (Dick) Punchard,
Son Neal and Daughter-in-law Isabelle,
Daughter Diane, and Son Evan.

Photographer - Gary Sherman

My thanks to Kiok Siem, Flora Jane Steffen,
Diane Punchard, and Isabelle Punchard for the
access of their collections plus Doris Diabo,
Ruth Liebing, June Nelson, Clara Schiller,
David Schuttleworth, Helga Stuewer, and Sue
Wagner for their sets. Thank you to the people
who helped translate foreign language material,
including Kiok & Han Siem, Isabelle Punchard,
Helga Stuewer, and Inga Douthitt.

Cover: "Christmas Party" by Maud Humphrey, 1894. This image was
used for a jigsaw puzzle. Courtesy of the Balliol Corporation.

Library of Congress Cataloging-in-Publication Data
Punchard, Lorraine May.
    Playtime pottery & porcelain. From Europe & Asia/Lorraine
Punchard.
        p. cm.
    Includes bibliographical references and index.
    ISBN 0-88740-974-1 (pbk)
    1. Miniature tableware--Collectors and collecting--Europe--
Catalogs. 2. Miniature tableware--Collectors and collecting--Asia--
Catalogs. I. Title.
NK8475.T33P876   1996
738'.0228--dc20   95-52684
                            CIP

Printed in Hong Kong
ISBN: 0-88740-974-1

Published by Schiffer Publishing Ltd.
77 Lower Valley Road
Atglen, PA 19310
Please write for a free catalog.
This book may be purchased from
the publisher.
Please include $2.95 for shipping.
Try your bookstore first.

Contents

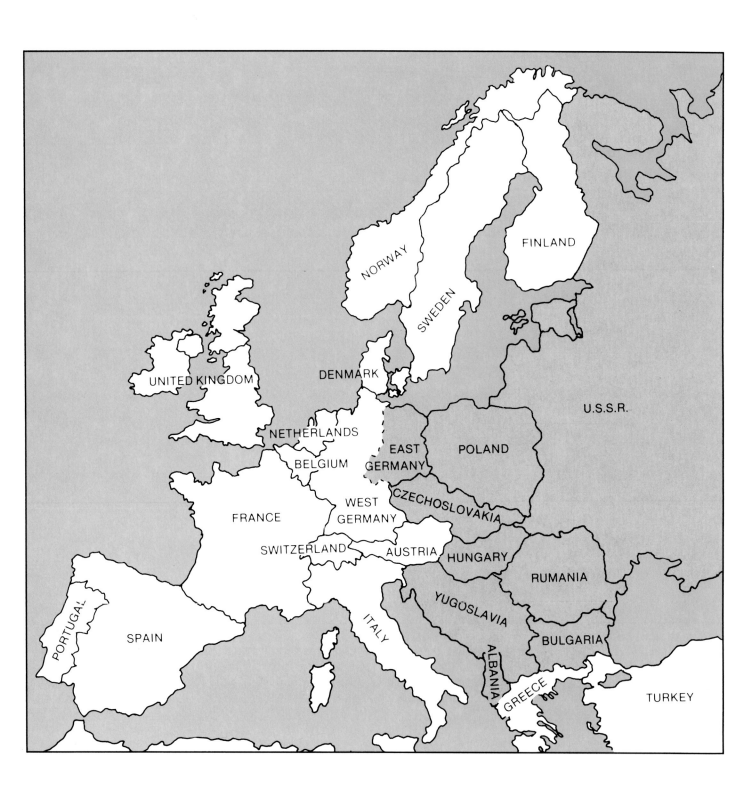

Map of Europe, the shaded area is eastern bloc. You can see the close proximity from one country to another. Distances were not far for workers to change jobs and carry their skills with them or for one pottery to copy examples from another pottery.

Introduction

The search for the factories that made children's dishes is never ending because other sets will always be surfacing. There is no way of knowing what companies made children's play dishes or how many, until sets are found and recorded. Most books on pottery and porcelain seldom mention children's pieces. It is surprising how many sets have survived, considering they were made as toys.

My purpose is to determine the country of origin of a piece by the shape of the mold, decoration, and material used, such as porcelain or pottery. Pottery is an earthenware that is fired and glazed. Other names used to describe pottery include semi-porcelain, soft-paste, opaque china, best body, new stone, and china stone. France uses the term half porcelain. To determine porcelain, hold a piece to the light and you will see your fingers through a translucent body, whereas earthenwares are opaque.

It is important to learn to compare shapes, sizes, covers, finials, embossing, and base rims to help determine the manufacturer and to date a set. One company could register a pattern and continue making it for many years, changing the decoration as often as they wished which makes it hard to match dishes made over one hundred years ago. Some earlier sets were not marked but as it became profitable the same company added their name to their product.

Many factories probably made these wares as a sideline, not attaching much importance to them. Over a century later, it is difficult to understand the problems of these companies. Some dishes were made from excess material, or by apprentice employees who may have used them for practice. In many cases, workmanship would not measure up to the quality of a particular factory, and if they were not intended for export they didn't have to be trademarked.

I have written to some companies that said they never made children's play dishes and then have found their mark on sets. Several circumstances could account for this. A company may have produced a few sets for sale but may not have included them in a catalog, or they could have been manufactured before good records were kept, or they may have been experimental sets. These sets may have been a special order or company personnel may have produced them for a family member. A company that had a well known mark was also sometimes copied by lesser known factories.

Early sets were often hand painted or hand painted over transfers. Transfers were applied by inking an engraved copper plate and stamping a tissue paper. Wet pigment was rubbed into clay wares, then soaked in water to remove the paper before firing. Glaze was applied over the transfers. This process has been used since the sixteenth century. Sometimes decoration was added by hand painting over the glaze. In later sets stenciling was applied through a cut-out pattern, which was simple to do and could use unskilled labor. Decals were also used. They were cut from a sheet, applied on the wares, and when fired the background disappeared. This was fast and did not require a lot of skill, like hand painting did. The advantage was the ability to create colorful decorations. In most cases the color of the mark has no significance. If it was a transfer, the mark was applied at the same time in the same color. A gold number was the mark of the gilder's, the decorator who applied the gold.

A nicely matched set includes cups and waste bowls with the same basic shape in different sizes. Another good point to remember in sizing features is that the height of the teapot is close to the diameter of the plates or saucers.

Blue Willow, by Mary Frank Gaston, identifies one hundred forty four marks that have been used on Willow wares from thirteen countries. Willow patterns are usually blue but they did come in other monochrome colors and even some polychrome colors.

Sets of children's play dishes were intended for a specific purpose, such as a tea set or a dinner service set, just as dishes were designed for adults. Their size depended on the intended use. Larger sets were meant to be used by little girls for having parties for their friends and practicing the social graces of the times. Smaller sets were made for little girls to have parties with their dolls, or for their dolls to have parties among themselves. Therefore, the smaller sizes were often referred to as "doll dishes." However, there is still a smaller size, usually referred to as miniature or doll house size. One standard doll house size is one inch to the foot.

According to the taste and means of a family, children's playtime dishes were a smaller scale of family china. Grading ranged from fair to exceptionally fine. An advertisement in the Butler Brothers catalog states that in 1890 you could buy china tea sets from five cents to five dollars. China toilet sets cost twenty-five cents to one dollar.

Dates of wars play an important role in the manufactured goods of a country. The United States imported large quantities of children's play dishes from Europe and England prior to World War 1 (1914 to 1918). Japan became the chief exporter of children's play dishes between the two World Wars, and again after World War II, which ended in 1945.

United States pottery companies produced sets from the late 1800s to World War I, with very few after that. The Akro Agate and Depression Glass companies manufactured glass sets for children's dishes during the 1930s and 1940s. Plastic has been the material used most since the 1950s.

Measurements given in descriptions are in decimals to the nearest 1/8 inch, because in many cases pieces will vary a little in the same set. Teapots are measured to the top of the finial. A finial is the top knob on covers of the serving pot and covers of the sugar bowl.

Notice the quality and interesting shapes of the sets pictured. Some are very fine in quality and craftsmanship, such as R.S. Prussia, while others were made with flaws and poor decorating which I am sure were intended to be used, played with, and ultimately broken. Finer sets would have been more of a teaching tool in Victorian times. This era reflects styles and customs in the years from about 1840 to 1890, particularly the Civil War period. When referring to a tea set of six place settings, articles included usually consisted of a teapot and cover, sugar bowl and cover, cream pitcher, six cups, six saucers, and six plates for a total of twenty-three pieces. English sets include a waste bowl for one additional piece. When a guest was served a second cup of tea, the remains in the cup were emptied into the waste bowl and fresh tea was served in the cup. It was never considered proper to add to the tea in one's cup. You may be wondering how many pieces came in a complete set. I'll try to explain by country as a rule, but there are always exceptions. Sets came in all sizes and number of pieces. Even at the turn of the twentieth century prices for a set must have had a range from about ten cents to ten dollars.

In 1891, Congress passed the McKinley Tariff Act. This required that goods imported to the United States be marked "Made In Country of Origin." Not every piece was marked and some used paper labels. To use the term "antique" an item should be at least one hundred years old, any less than that are considered collectibles.

The United States of America has imported quantities of dishes from England, Germany, France, and Japan. All the other countries have been difficult to collect. Looking at a map of Europe, you can see the closeness of the countries and as the artists and workers in the ceramic trade moved from one factory to another, they carried their skills with them. It could have been within their own country or another country as they are close in proximity. You can see the similarities in the European and Scandinavian ceramics in both the base materials and the shapes.

Estimate prices are for the prices pictured in mint condition. This is only a guide. Prices are determined by supply and demand and may vary in different areas of the country. Prices should be lower for any missing pieces, chips, cracks, or repairs.

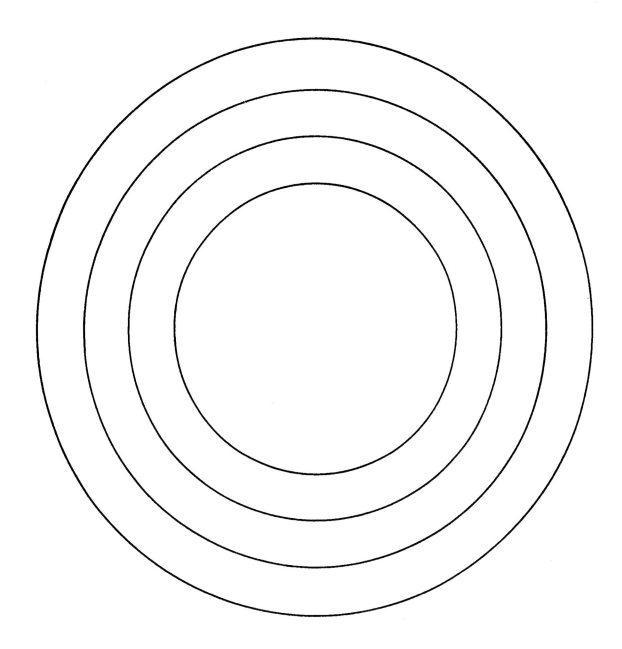

This guide is for saucers and plates 3, 4, 5, & 6 inches in diameter.

Plates 4 to 5 inches in diameter are typical sizes for the children's play dishes.

English plates are usually in the four to five inch catagory.

German plates tend to run a little larger, often 5.25 to 5.5 inches.

Doll dishes are usually 3 inches and smaller.

Austria

Pottery and porcelain toy dishes were produced in Austria in the nineteenth and twentieth century. Carisbad was known as Karisbad after World War I when that section of Austria became part of Czechoslovakia. This area was a center for porcelain factories.

"Victoria : Austria" is from the porcelain factory Victoria Schmidt & Co. that was in business from 1883 to 1945. The little sugar bowl is fine porcelain with a soft floral decal. The edges are trimmed in gold. Single pieces are not usually included, but the mark is important and maybe someone has a full set. The size of the sugar bowl is 1.75 inches high and 3.25 inches to the outsides of the handles. $25-50.

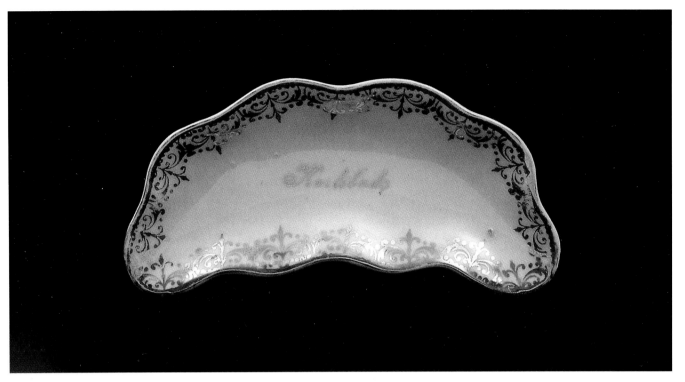

"M Z, AUSTRIA" is the trademark for Moritz Zdekauer. The factory at Altrohlau was in business from 1884 to 1909. This little bone dish is white porcelain with gold trim. Bone dishes were shaped to fit around the dinner plate. They were used for bone remains from the meal. The name "Kaslsbach" is printed on the face of the piece which appears to be a souvenir piece. I have not yet seen a child's dinner set that includes bone dishes. However, taking into account all the things that were made for children's play, someone may run across this oddity. The bone dish size is 2 by 4.5 inches. $25-50.

These two Austrian tea sets match the following dinner service set. The same transfers are on all three sets. Some pieces have the impressed beehive mark and many pieces are not marked at all. They came from Europe so they did not need to have a trademark. Each set $300-400.
  Teapot with cover 4.5" high and 3.5" high,
  Open sugar bowl with both sets,
  Creamer with the small set,
  Five cups & five saucers 4.25" diameter,
  Three cups & three saucers 3.5" diameter.

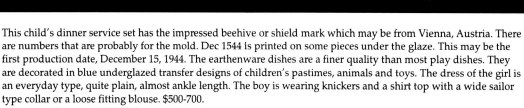

This child's dinner service set has the impressed beehive or shield mark which may be from Vienna, Austria. There are numbers that are probably for the mold. Dec 1544 is printed on some pieces under the glaze. This may be the first production date, December 15, 1944. The earthenware dishes are a finer quality than most play dishes. They are decorated in blue underglazed transfer designs of children's pastimes, animals and toys. The dress of the girl is an everyday type, quite plain, almost ankle length. The boy is wearing knickers and a shirt top with a wide sailor type collar or a loose fitting blouse. $500-700.

A covered tureen, 4.75" high,
An offset butter boat with attached tray,
Platter 5.5 by 8",
Large, medium & small open serving dishes,
Large serving plate 5.5" diameter,
Six dinner plates 5.5" diameter,
Six smaller plates 5 " diameter.

Small mugs and pitchers are typical pottery wares from Austria. The pottery was usually a buff color with different design decorations and colors. The pieces pictured are brown but blue was also used. The sizes range from doll house pieces, doll dishes to children's play dishes. The mugs are approximately 1.25 inches high, and the saucers are 2.37 inches in diameter. Each piece $35-65.

"AUSTRIA" is impressed on the pitcher and bowl. The decorating is Sgraffito in color tan with dark brown lines and bars. The pitcher is 3 inches high and the bowl top diameter is 4 inches. $100-200.

"AUSTRIA" is stamped on the bottom of this pottery set. The pottery is cream color with blue glaze and trim. The checkerboard design is cream color and blue. It is an inexpensive twentieth century play set. This type of decorating is called Sgraffito. It is cut-through slip applied to the body before glazing to reveal the body beneath. $150-250.

Teapot with cover 5" high,
Creamer & open sugar bowl,
Two cups & two saucers 3.5" diameter.

"Snow White And The Seven Dwarfs" was a popular fairy tale that was used in decorating children's play dishes. This earthenware set has the impressed beehive trademark circa 1920s. The main decal pictures Snow White and Prince Charming. The smaller decals are from scenes in the story. The cups are small mug shape. *Courtesy of Flora Jane Steffen.* $600-800.

Teapot with cover 4.25" high,
Creamer & open sugar bowl,
Six cups & six saucers 3.12" diameter.

"GEMMA" is printed in a shield with a crown on this little dresser set. It is credited to Schmidt & Co., Victoria, Austria, after 1904. It is porcelain decorated with crests and a name in the banner. The tray, 3 by 4.5 inches, and candlestick, 2.75 inches high, include the names "PORTA MARIS PORTUS SALUTIS" and below that "BOROUGH ARMS MARGATE." The other four pieces have "DOMINS DIRIGE NOS." They include a tall covered jar, two short covered jars, and a small pitcher. $150-250.

Another rare porcelain item is a child's desk set. It is trademarked "VICTORIA, CARLSBAD, AUSTRIA" dating 1890 to 1918. The decals are little Cupids and flowers. It includes four corner pieces to fit the desk pad which is 9.5 by 15 inches, an open dish to hold the pens, an ink well, a hand blotter, a sponge dish, and a stamp dish. It is a beautiful porcelain set and every collector would like one. *Courtesy of Ruth Liebing.* $900-1200.

Belgium

In Belgium, porcelain factories were located in Brussels and other locations with no mention of children's toy dishes in the reference books.

    This Belgium set was purchased as coming from Nimy or the seat of the "Master School for Ceramics." The school encouraged ceramic technique and individual artistic expression. It would date 1880 to 1890. The set is earthenware with brown transfers. Colors are hand painted over the transfers but under the glaze. It has a narrow border. Each saucer includes three or four small transfers of children, animals, or toys. The large scenes include a woman holding a baby with two small children watching; and a man sitting on a bench smoking with a boy sitting on a stool. It is quite unusual for a tea set to come with twelve cups and saucers. $700-900.

  Teapot with cover 5.5" high,
  Covered sugar bowl,
  Twelve cups & twelve saucers 3.5" diameter.

Belgium is the country that made these child's size plates. These were purchased at antique shows and it is not known if they came with a toy tea set. The decor is perfect for children. They appear to be early twentieth century pieces.

One earthenware plate is decorated with a transfer of a goat standing in a field by a fence. The color is red to pink luster. The trademark reads "NIMY, MADE IN BELGIUM."

The two blue earthenware plates are decorated with the scene of a Dutch boy and girl, with a background of sailboats, sitting on a bench drinking tea. Floral designs complete the background. The trademark reads "BY BOCH, BELGIUM, DELFTS."

The plates are 4.5 inches in diameter. Each plate $20-25.

Opposite page photo:
This picture is from the Sotheby Parke Bernet, Inc. auction catalog of the Garbisch Collection held in 1980. The descriptions are taken from the catalog.

Top: "Fine and rare Chinese Export child's part tea and coffee service, 1795-1800, comprising a teapot, cover and stand, a milk jug, a spoon tray, four coffee cups, two teabowls, and four saucers; each piece colorfully painted with a scene of two little girls watching two boys playing marbles in a hilly landscape, the rims with iron-red, blue and gilt borders of florettes, lines, dots, and husks. 14 pieces. Height of teapot 3.87 inches."

Center: "Chinese Export child's part tea and coffee service, circa 1800, comprising a teapot, cover and stand, a milk jug and cover, a tea caddy, a spoon tray, two coffee cups, two teabowls and two saucers; similarly decorated to the following lot within slightly barbed rims. 11 pieces. Height of teapot 4 inches."

Bottom: "Chinese Export child's part tea and coffee service, circa 1800, comprising a teapot, cover and stand, a tea caddy, a spoon tray, two coffee cups, two teabowls and four saucers; each piece colorfully painted with a little girl and boy leaving home for school, their mother in the doorway behind within a gold and blue husk rounded and gold and blue band and feathery spearhead borders. 12 pieces. Height of teapot 3.87 inches."

China

Chinese Export is a term used to describe the Chinese porcelain wares that came from China. These wares were made for export and are different from the wares that were made for their home market. The shapes were often copies of European or English silver. The color of the porcelain has a gray tint with tiny pits in the surface.

The Portuguese began trade in 1556. In 1602 the Dutch East India Company was founded and traded with China. The English began trade with China in 1631, and the first ship to trade under the American Flag was the *Empress of China* in 1784. The Americans brought furs, coins, lead, cloth, and herb ginseng trading them for tea, spices, silks, and porcelain. The first cargo included 64 tons of porcelain and 342 chests of tea which served as ballast. The ship also contained spices and textiles. From 1784 to about 1835, the United States imported wares directly from China. The European trade continued to expand and was at its highest between 1760 and 1780. By this time the Meissen factory in Germany learned to make porcelain. It was then copied by numerous factories including Bow, Chelsea, and Derby in England.

Many export wares were decorated to order of the merchants. If a ship captain brought an order, he would pick it up the next time he returned, about two years later. This is why sets are found decorated with initials, Coats of Arms, and Crests, and may be referred to as armorial porcelains.

Due to political problems, trade with China was closed for many years in the 20th century. President Nixon began to re-open trade with China in 1969. In 1971 some goods were approved for export. Trade agreements were still being worked out in 1973.

The Cherry Pickers' is taken from a print. "Fine Chinese Export 'Cherry Pickers' small teabowl and saucer, 1775-1785." The saucer diameter is 2.62 inches.

This white porcelain Chinese Export toy tea set has fancy scroll initials that look like M.R. The date would be circa 1780 to 1790. The teapot is globular with a loop handle. The original cover must have been broken or lost and someone had a silver cover made to fit the teapot. There is applied decoration on the handle. The sugar bowl is flared at the top. The tea caddy was used to store dry tea. It would originally have had a cover. There are four deep dish saucers. Some early sets came with tea bowls and cups with one set of saucers because you would be serving either tea or coffee and would only need one set of saucers. $3000-4000.

Teapot with silver cover 3.75" high,
Creamer & open sugar bowl,
Tea caddy 3.25" high, 2" wide,
Four tea bowls & four cups,
Four saucers 3.62" diameter.

Opposite page, bottom:
This toy set of porcelain dishes has fancy initials that look like L.R. This would mean the dishes were made to order for this family through a merchant. The red and blue trim is under the glaze and the gold is over the glaze. It would date circa 1785 to 1795. The set contains a drum shaped tea pot with a straight spout, double-twisted handles and a cover with a bud finial. The sugar bowl has a wide lid that fits over the top with the same double-twisted handles and bud finial. The creamer is helmet shape. The covered dish with an underplate is probably a Bon-Bon dish with a tea set. The cups are mug shape rather than a tea bowl shape. $3000-4000.

Teapot with cover 3.87" high,
Teapot stand 4.5" diameter,
Creamer & covered sugar bowl,
One serving dish 4.5" diameter,
One Bon-Bon dish with stand,
Four cups & four saucers 4.25" diameter.

This Chinese Export set is dated later than the two previous sets, circa 1830. The porcelain has a gray tone with a few tiny pits. It is beautifully hand painted with flowers, leaves, berries, exotic birds and many varieties of butterflies and bugs. The teapot is drum shaped with a cover that fits nicely. It has a nut finial. The sugar bowl is large with a cover that fits over the top, and the finial matches the teapot finial. Both pieces have double twisted handles. This is a service for eight. $2300-2700.

Teapot with cover 4" high.

Covered sugar bowl

Eight cups & eight saucers 4.75" diameter.

This Chinese Export tea bowl and saucer are the style of about 1785. The porcelain pieces have been handcrafted and aren't exactly even. The decoration is all hand painted. The outside edge is bittersweet, then cobalt blue with gold outline and trim was added. The urn with flowers uses the same colors. The tea bowl is 2 inches in diameter by 1.25" high. The saucer diameter is 3.75 inches. $100-200.

These two Chinese Export porcelain tea bowls and saucers include hand painted enameled flowers, leaves, and butterflies for decoration. The tea bowls have a finely executed base. These pieces represent the style of about 1785. Both the tea bowls and saucers have fine ribbing. These are the only pieces to this set. The saucers are 3.5 inches in diameter. $150-250.

This novelty tea pot would be a mass produced novelty article dating after 1973. It is marked "MADE IN CHINA." It is quite heavy and painted with unskilled labor. The elephant tea pot has a baby elephant finial. It is 5.25 inches high and 7.25 inches from the tip of the spout to the outside of the handle. $25-50.
The smaller blue and white elephant tea pot is quite new. The novelty teapot is white with a dark blue painted elephant, decoration and handles. Even the trunks are painted on. The finial is in the shape of a baby elephant. The teapot is not marked but the box that it came in was marked "MADE IN CHINA." The teapot is 3.75 inches high. $25-50.

"FISHEL TOYS, Made in China" is printed on the box. Other information on the box reads "16 PCS FINE PORCELAIN TEA SET, Includes: teapot with lid, creamer and sugar bowl, 4 cake plates, and 4 cups and saucers." The china pieces are marked with a paper label "MADE IN CHINA." It was new in 1994 for the price of fifteen dollars. It is heavy porcelain, all machine molded. $15-20.

 Teapot with cover 3" high,
 Creamer & open sugar bowl,
 Four plates 3.5" diameter.
 Four cups & four saucers 2.75" diameter.

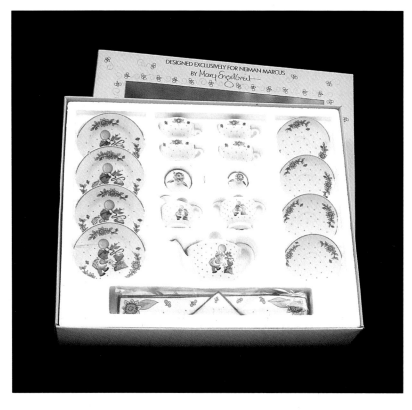

Taiwan is the Chinese name for the island we used to call Formosa. It is located off the southeast coast of China. Each year the Neiman Marcus store sells a porcelain set of children's dishes. This 1991 set came from Taiwan. It was decorated with decals of two little bears, dressed as children, one pouring tea and one holding a cup. Flowers, leaves, and bees decorated the borders. $75-100. The information on the box is:
"Designed Exclusively for Neiman Marcus
by Mary Engelbreit
Seventeen Piece Toy Tea Set
4 Plates • 4 Cups and Saucers • 1 Teapot with lid
1 Sugar Bowl with lid • 1 Cream Pitcher
Four Place Mats and Four Napkins
Made In Taiwan R.O.C."

 Teapot with lid 3.25" high,
 Creamer & covered sugar bowl,
 Four plates 4.5" diameter,
 Four cups & four saucers 3.75" diameter.

Czechoslovakia

In 1918, after the first World War, Bohemia, Slovakia, and Silesia formed an independent republic whose name is now Czecholsovakia. Therefore any pottery or porcelain marked Czechoslovakia would date after 1918. The dishes range from finely crafted porcelain, to earthenwares, to a heavy crude pottery.

"VICTORIA CHINA CZECHOSLOVAKIA" is the trademark on this set of fine porcelain. Victoria China was produced at Altrohlau, Bohemia, formerly part of Austria. It was listed as making keepsakes and utility wares. This porcelain set, circa 1930, is decorated in a Christmas theme. The decals include a Christmas tree, bells with holly, candles, and an elf stirring food. $500-700.

Teapot with cover 6" high,
Creamer & covered sugar bowl,
Five cups & five saucers 4" diameter.

"VICTORIA, CZECHOSLOVAKIA" is marked on this small dinner service set. It was not made for the American market so it does not contain the words "Made In." This set is a fine porcelain dinner service set decorated with brightly colored modern designs. $200-300.

A covered serving dish 3" high,
One platter 3 by 4",
Six plates 3.12" diameter.

CZECHO-SLOVAKIA

"CZECHOSLOVAKIA" is impressed on this very crude heavy pottery tea set. It is decorated with a rough drawing of a house and green bushes. It looks as if unskilled labor was used. This same type of crude dinnerware also came decorated with chickens. Sets made from different batches have darker or lighter paint. $100-150.

Teapot with cover 5" high,
Creamer & covered sugar bowl,
Serving dish 4.25" square,
Two plates 4.87" diameter,
Two cups & two saucers 3.5" diameter.

Another set marked "CZECHOSLOVAKIA" in heavy crude pottery is decorated with a little dog. The trim on this set is of a dog standing on grass and is a bit raised. The other trim is green leaves and red berries. There is an unusual combination of pieces that include the teapot, creamer, and sugar bowl for a tea service and four serving pieces for a dinner set. *Courtesy of Flora Jane Steffen.* $200-300.

Teapot with cover 3.5" high,
Creamer & covered sugar bowl,
Tureen with underplate,
Open serving bowl 4 inch diameter,
Square serving dish 4.25",
Large serving plate 5.5" diameter.

Czechoslovakia is the country of origin for this tea set. It is brown glazed earthenware with hand painted raised design in red and yellow. It is not a quality set, but an inexpensive toy. The covers do not fit evenly. The teapot is small for the size of the other pieces. The country name is impressed on the bottom of the plates and saucers. Any dishes marked Czechoslovakia would date after 1918 when the independent republic was formed. $150-250.

Teapot with cover 5" high,
Creamer & covered sugar bowl,
Four plates 5" diameter,
Four cups & four saucers 3.5" diameter.

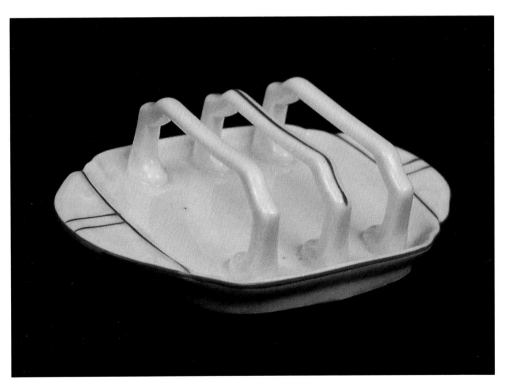

"Victoria" with a crown is trademarked on the toast rack. It is beautifully made and decorated with a blue line trim. The base is 2.87 by 4.5 inches. *Courtesy of Flora Jane Steffen.* $50-75.

Denmark

Denmark's industrialization escalated in the 1870s. One of Denmark's advantages was their trading sea port center, located between Scandinavia and Germany with shipping routes around the world. The two major porcelain factories are Royal Copenhagen and Bing & Grondahl. Bing & Grondahl was established in 1853 by the M. Ludwig Brothers, Harold Bing and Frederick V. Grondahl. At this time no information is available that they made children's toy dishes.

"Royal Copenhagen" is a well known porcelain factory in Denmark established in 1760. The term "Royal" means by royal appointment. The three wavy lines symbolize the three ancient waterways from the Kattegat to the Baltic. By 1867 "Royal" was a courtesy title. In 1884 Philip Schou bought the factory and moved it to Smallegade. Their work includes underglaze and overglaze painting. The company is known for its figurines and vases as well as dinnerware. This ever popular design is called "Blue Fluted." These pieces have been assembled separately to form a partial set. They are fine porcelain, all trademarked. The cookie dish dates between 1894 and 1922. The other pieces with "Denmark" added date after 1923. $700-900.

Teapot with cover 4.12" high,
Cream pitcher,
Cookie dish 4.12" diameter,
Four plates 4.12" diameter.

Royal Copenhagen used the trademark on this set between 1923 and 1929. It is nicely molded with a fine glaze. The color is shaded tones of blue. It is a floral design with cobalt finials. $700-900.

Teapot with cover 6.25" high,
Creamer & covered sugar bowl,
Two cups & two saucers 3.5" diameter.

Denmark is said to be the country of origin of this set. It is not marked and is open for discussion. It is a modern set made as an inexpensive toy. The base color is reddish-brown pottery with heavy white glaze. It is decorated with hand painted flowers and pink bands. $75-125.

Teapot with cover 4.87" high,
Three cups & three saucers 4 " diameter.

25

Finland

Finland had strong influences and rule from Sweden and Russia. In 1906 the parliamentary system was reformed and Finland began to improve its economic situation.

The Arabia porcelain factory is located in a suburb of Helsinki, Finland. The name came from a nineteenth century villa in Helsinki that was built by a general who had lived in the Arabian countries. Arabia was founded in 1874 by the Swedish Company, Rorstrand, and in 1916 began as a cooperative. They made table and decorative wares in standard European style. Transfer prints were supplied by the Swedish Company, Rorstrand. In 1900, Arabia exhibited ceramics at the International Exhibit in Paris. The company employs many artists who are given a free hand to create and decorate their wares. They are a leader in their field of ceramics. This large factory produces both porcelain and earthenware in a wide range of products. They have used a series of marks that accurately date their wares.

The Arabia factory made this tea set. It is trademarked, dating it 1917 to 1927. The set is earthenware with fine smooth glaze, and no crazing. It is decorated with decals of black silhouette children playing with kites or a paper lantern in red, yellow, or blue. The rims are trimmed in gold. The mold shape is the same as sets from Sweden. $800-1000.

Teapot with cover 5.75" high,
Creamer & covered sugar bowl,
Twelve cups & twelve saucers 4" diameter.

"ARABIA, MADE IN FINLAND" is trade-marked on the four little plates dating them 1964 to 1971. They are fine quality, decorated with scenic pictures of spring, summer, fall, and winter. The scenes include a woman selling at an outdoor market, two men rolling logs in the river, two girls with an umbrella on a windy day, and two little girls skiing and pulling a sled. They are 3.75 inches in diameter. $50-75.

♕
ARABIA
MADE IN
FINLAND

The same Arabia trademark as the preceding set is on this little hot pad. The earthenware piece is decorated with blue transfers. The border has flowers and leaves, a castle is pictured in the center. It is 3.25 inches in diameter. $35-50.

The third example with the same Arabia trademark is on a cup and saucer. It is earthenware with fine glazing, decorated with red transfer in floral and leaf design. The saucer is 4 inches in diameter. $35-50.

Large kaolin deposits were discovered in Saint-Yrieix-la-Perche near Limoges in the year 1768. The pits supplied kaolin to Sèvres, as well as Strasbourg, France; Frankenthal, Germany; Nymphenburg, Germany; and Copenhagen, Denmark.

The map locates main pottery and porcelain centers in France.

France

French hard paste porcelain is nonporous. The kaolin, white clay ingredient, and feldspar (feldspathic rock) is molded, fired at a high temperature, then glaze is applied and fired at a still higher temperature. This procedure fuses the glaze into the body to create a delicate looking, translucent porcelain. The spoilage in this method is higher than glazed pottery thus making it more expensive to make.

The most notable characteristic feature of early French porcelain is the pure white color. There were quite a number of porcelain factories around Paris from the late eighteenth century and all through the nineteenth century. These wares are also referred to as Old Paris china and are seldom marked. They had fine clays and the factories could produce quality wares. The majority of toy sets date from about the middle of the nineteenth century.

In the late nineteenth and early twentieth century French makers produced a wide range of sets using material from pure white porcelain to faience. The wares range from beautifully crafted porcelain to inexpensive toy dishes. In France earthenwares or semi-porcelain are referred to as half porcelain. Besides the range of materials there is a wide variation in the shapes and sizes by numerous china producing companies. Sizes range from small doll dishes to large services for little girls to use while eating a meal. Another French custom featured display packaging including items such as table flatware, glassware, and napkins to use in conjunction with a tea service or dinner service. Most of the tureens do not have a cutout in the lid for the handle of the soup ladle. The packaging in wooden display boxes was common before the First World War in 1914. After the war the boxes were usually cardboard.

Limoges is a city in France known for its porcelain factories. Limoges wares were white porcelain usually sold as white ware to be decorated elsewhere. Quite often a mark will include "Limoges, France" and another mark would be the decorator. This is a standard practice and is still common today.

Other well known names associated with toy dishes include Sarreguemines, Lunéville, and Choisy LeRoi.

French Tea Sets

"MONTEREAU" and "L L" is impressed on some pieces. Some of the earliest toy dishes came from the city of Montereau, France. L.L. stands for Louis Leboeuf who was one of the owners. A faience factory was founded here in 1796. There is a family and children's series, some of which are used to decorate this child's toy set.

This wonderful set, circa 1815 to 1825, has bright yellow glaze with black transfers and black hand painted rims. The transfers include a boy with a big dog in four separate scenes; a boy with an animal in a cage; a girl chasing a butterfly; a girl talking to a parrot; and a man on a horse. The teapot is drum-shaped with a dome cover. The cups are flared and include handles. The saucers are like small bowls. $1800-2200.

Teapot with cover 3.62" high,
Covered sugar bowl,
Waste bowl,
One plate 4.5" diameter,
Two cups & two saucers 3.5" diameter.

Sèvres is a French factory that was founded in 1753 and moved to Sèvres in 1756. It had royal ownership with hired directors managing the factory. They made hard paste porcelain in the finest quality and decorating. From 1804 to 1815 orders for the Emperor Napoleon kept the factory busy. As directors and artistic managers changed, so did the work at Sèvres. The Sèvres mark has a continuous loop on each side, the trademark with a Y would date 1776. This is a version of a Sèvres trademark used to confuse the public. It is Old Paris porcelain made to look like Sèvres in style, decorating, and trademark. It would date from about 1870 to 1890. It is porcelain decorated with hand painted enamel flowers and heavy gold trim. The flowers are rose, lavender, blue, and red with green leaves. The gold trim is on the rims, handles, spouts, and finials. $500-700.

    Tray 6.5" square,
    Teapot 2.5" high,
    Chocolate pot 3.25" high,
    One cup & one saucer 3.25" diameter.

French Old Paris dishes sometimes have a thick porcelain base unlike any other china from other countries. This unique set has many special features beside the thick base, such as a serpent style teapot spout, a tall creamer with a wide squared lip, and a large round sugar bowl. The decorations of vertical lines and flowers are hand painted over the glaze and finished with gold trim. $400-600.

    Teapot with cover 5" high,
    Creamer & covered sugar bowl,
    Four cups & four saucers 4.12" diameter.

Old Paris French porcelain is pure white and is seldom marked. The bases of the serving pieces have thick porcelain unglazed on the bottom surface. This set has lovely shapes with ornate handles and ample gold trim, characteristic of wares from about 1870 to 1880s. The set is finely hand painted with little fish on a blue background. Around the fish are stems, leaves, and flowers. $400-600.

    Teapot with cover 3.5" high
    Creamer & covered sugar bowl,
    Six plates 3.62" diameter,
    Six cups & six saucers 3.5" diameter.

This is another fine example of beautiful white Old Paris porcelain. It has hand painted flowers in pink and purple with stems and green leaves. All the pieces have wonderful embossing. There is gold accent trim on some of the embossing and on the ornate handles as well as gold rims. The porcelain bases are thick. *Courtesy of Sue Wagner.* $500-700.

    Teapot with cover 5" high,
    Creamer & covered sugar bowl,
    Six plates 5" diameter,
    Six cups & six saucers 4.62" diameter.

Notice the shapes of this typically French design. This style was used in adult sets then copied for children's toys. It could also be called Old Paris china. This small pure white porcelain set is decorated with hand painted flowers, gold trim, and gold French words written on the face of the pieces. They include "Désir," Desire; "Joie," Joy; "Paix," Peace; "Bonté," Goodness; "Beauté," Beauty; and "Amour," Love. The sugar bowl has a wide opening with a large cover fitting over the top. The cream pitcher has a wide squared lip to match the design of the set. $200-300.

Teapot with cover 3.75" high,
Creamer & covered sugar bowl,
Five cups & five saucers 2.75" diameter.

The second set with the same style shape is hand painted with blue dots and dashes, pink flowers and green leaves with an Oriental design. This set is small doll size. The cup handle is a butterfly design. $200-300.

Teapot with cover 2.87" high,
Creamer & covered sugar bowl,
One cup & one saucer 2.5" diameter.

"H" is marked in dark blue. Hannong established a hard paste porcelain factory in Paris, at the Faubourg St. Denis in 1769. This set would date from about 1870 or later. "H" may stand for a family member who continued to use this mark or it could be an unknown factory that copied the fine type of work and mark of this factory. The porcelain has a beautiful pure white smooth finish with cobalt blue flowers. The small hand painted flowers are shades of pink with green leaves. It is finished with heavily decorated gold trim. The teapot is tall with a serpent spout and dome cover, the creamer is tall with a wide lip. $400-600.

   Teapot with cover 4.12" high,
   Creamer & covered sugar bowl,
   Small bowl,
   Six cups & six saucers 3.37" diameter.

This set has a mold similar to the preceding set but is decorated only with gold trim. It could also be called early Paris and dates from about 1870 and later. The outstanding features are the pure milky white porcelain decorated with a large quantity of gold trim that has been skillfully applied. The size could be considered large doll dishes. $400-600.

   Teapot with cover 4" high,
   Creamer & covered sugar bowl,
   Five cups & five saucers 3.25" diameter.

Right:
Bordeaux is a large city in France that produced fine porcelain tea sets. The Royal manufacturer of porcelains sold under the name porcelain of Saxe. French "Prov" could mean "Provenance" (coming from Saxe) or "Province" (province). This set may have come from this area after 1870. It is porcelain with cobalt blue decorations that include a bird in the design. Gold rims and gold gilding over the blue complete the decoration. $400-600.

    Teapot with cover 5.37" high,
    Creamer & covered sugar bowl,
    Six cups & six saucers 3.5" diameter.

A wooden display box holds this fine porcelain tea set marked "T, 5." The T may stand for the city of Lorient, France. The 5 could be the decorator's identification number or the date 1905. This is a fine porcelain set decorated with cobalt blue then hand painted with red flowers and green leaves. Gold gilding enhances the colors on this fine quality set. $700-900.

    Teapot with cover 4" high,
    Creamer & covered sugar bowl,
    Six cups & six saucers 2.5" diameter.

This small doll-sized tea set came in the original cardboard box, including six 2.5 inch pewter spoons. It is porcelain decorated with little hand painted pink flowers and green leaves. It would date about 1890 to 1910. The box size is 4.25 by 6.5 inches. $500-700.

    Teapot with cover 2.62" high,
    Creamer & covered sugar bowl,
    Six cups & six saucers 2" diameter.

French hard paste porcelain is a pure white nonporous body which was used to make this fine toy set. It is decorated with heavy gold trim. The inside top portion of the pieces are shaded light pink. It could be called Old Paris and would date after 1870. $400-600.

    Teapot with cover 4" high,
    Creamer & sugar bowl,
    Two cups & two saucers 3.62" diameter.

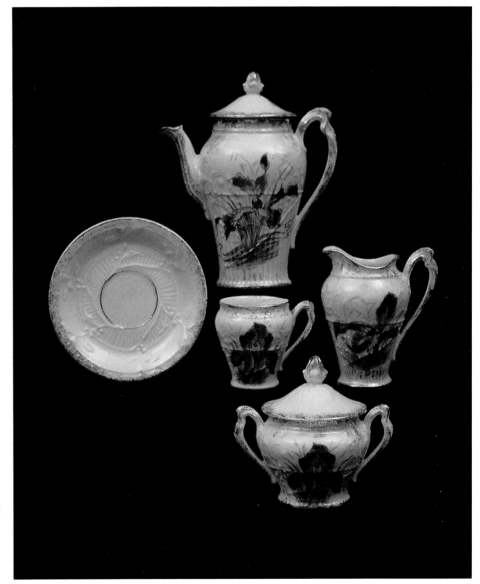

Fine porcelain with exceptional embossed designs on all the pieces makes this mold special. It would date late nineteenth century. The embossing includes ridges and stems with flowers and leaves. The hand painted decorations are purple irises with yellow centers and green leaves. Gold trim decorates all the edges. *Courtesy of Isabelle Punchard.* $700-900.

    Teapot with cover 5.5" high,
    Creamer & covered sugar bowl,
    Four cups & four saucers 4" diameter.

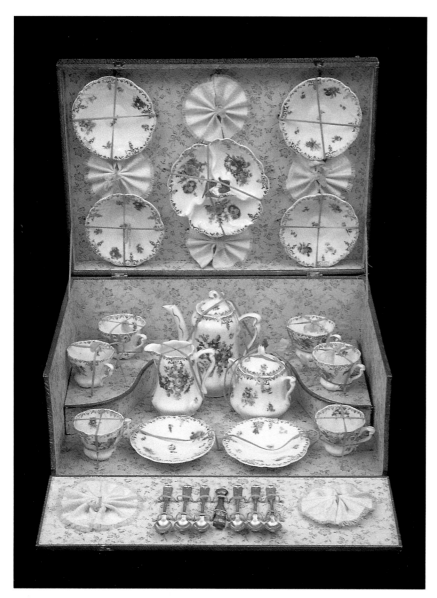

"SERVICE THÉ" is written on the cover of the French wooden box. The paper is green made to look like simulated leather. The brass latches have the initials G.M. Inside the box is a lovely, fine quality porcelain tea set. It is beautifully molded with thin porcelain cups. It is trademarked "PROV. SAXE, E.S." The porcelain was made in Suhl, Prussia, by Erdmann Schlegelmilch. He was part of the RS Prussia family making fine porcelains. The factory began in 1861, this set would date between 1880 and 1910. The mark is a German trademark sold in a French box. $800-1000.

   Teapot with cover 5.75" high,
   Creamer & covered sugar bowl,
   Three section serving dish 5.5" diameter,
   Six cups & six saucers 4.25" diameter,
   Six napkins,
   Six pewter spoons and tin sugar tongs.

This French tea set is nice porcelain decorated with pink bands, hand painted flowers and gold trim. It would date around 1890 or later. The saucers are deep with no rims for the bases of the cups. This is the beginning of a style that was used for numerous sets of toy dishes. It is of a finer quality than later sets. $400-600.

   Teapot with cover 6.12" high,
   Covered sugar bowl,
   Six plates 4.25" diameter,
   Six cups & six saucers 4.25" diameter.

Typical base styles include this average toy tea set. It has the shape and size from about the 1890s to the first World War in 1914. It is decorated with hand painted flowers and gold trim. $300-400.

Teapot with cover 3.87" high,
Creamer & covered sugar bowl,
Four cups & four saucers 3" diameter.

This set of toy dishes is similar to the preceding set in style and dating. The pieces are not trademarked but they most likely came in a presentation box that had a label. They are white porcelain of average quality decorated with a gold band trim. $250-350.

Teapot with cover 4.62" high,
Creamer & covered sugar bowl,
Four cups & four saucers 3.25" diameter.

"L.J & CIE, FRANCE, VIERZON" are all impressed markings on this tea set. Vierzon is a city in France. Porcelain is used to make this attractive set in the Art Deco style of the 1920s and 1930s. The cups and saucers have octagon ridges while the serving pieces are flat. The decoration includes flower decals and hand painted blue line trim. $300-400.

Teapot with cover 5.25" high,
Creamer & covered sugar bowl,
Four cups & four saucer 3.75" diameter.

Above:
French porcelain came in a wide variety of styles. This set has especially interesting handles with raised dots and gold trim. All the decorations are hand painted in soft colors making this an attractive set. $300-400.

 Teapot with cover 4.75" high,
 Creamer & covered sugar bowl,
 Six plates 4.5" diameter,
 Six cups & six saucers 4.12" diameter.

Right:
"Porcelaine, Cérabel" is on the back stamp for the maker. It is child-size but may have been intended as an individual service. The face of the pieces read, "Patisserie Moderne, M. Lobelle-Dauchy, YPRÉS." It means Modern Pastry Shop. The center banner is the name of the owners, and at the bottom Yprés is the city. Between the lettering is a picture of a pastry. $100-200.

 Teapot with cover 3.25" high,
 Cream pitcher.

PORCELAINE Cérabel

"LIMOGES, CHANCE, L. SAZERAT, MADE FOR W. DONALDSON & CO., MINNE-APOLIS" is on the trademark. Limoges is the city where the porcelain was made. Léon Sazerat, Blondeau & Co., managed a decorating studio in Limoges from 1884 to 1893. W. Donaldson & Co. was a large department store located in Minneapolis, Minnesota. These serving porcelain pieces are bulbous with fine hand painted flowers and gold trim. $100-200.

 Teapot with cover 4.75" high,
 Creamer & covered sugar bowl.

Sarreguemines used this trademark after 1910. The shapes are oval with a straight spout on the teapot. The cream pitcher matches the shape. The cups have straight sides that fit into the metal holders. All the pieces are pure white porcelain with nickel-plated brass metal moldings. $300-500.

Teapot with cover 4.5" high,
Creamer pitcher 3" high,
Four cups.

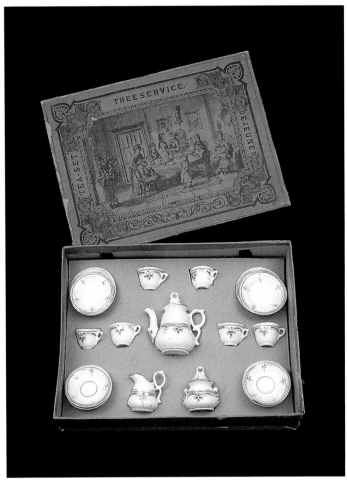

Left and Above:
Both of these sets were found in their original boxes with similar lithograph covers. The style of dress on these boxes date them from the 1880s to the 1890s. Both sets include "TEA-SET, THEE SERVICE, DÉJEUNER." This means a lunch set. The large box has small letters "DEP. G. Z. is., A.E. lith." The small box has small letters "DEPONIRT, S & T." This type of set in a cardboard box would date about 1890 to 1915. It is typical of the inexpensive wares produced as common toys. It is pencilled on one side $1.00. The sets are molded and hand painted with low quality control. The plates and saucers are all uneven. Each set $300-500.

Teapot with cover 4" high	Teapot with cover 3.25" high
Creamer & covered sugar bowl	Creamer & covered sugar bowl,
Six plates 3.5" diameter,	Six plates 2.5" diameter,
Six cups & six saucers 3.12" diameter.	Six cups & six saucers 2.37" diam.

"K. G., DEMI-PORCELAINE, LUNÉVILLE, MADE IN FRANCE" is the information on the trademark. Demi-Porcelaine means half porcelain (earthenware). After 1788 K and G are on the trademark which stands for Keller & Guérin, along with the location name Lunéville. The term "Made In France" would date this set after 1891. It is decorated with quality hand painted flowers and leaves. The teapot finial is decorated as a piece of fruit. $100-200.

    Teapot with cover 5.12" high,
    Cream pitcher,
    One serving plate 6.25" diameter,
    One cup & one saucer 4.5" diameter.

"K. G., MÉSANGE, LUNÉVILLE" is on the trademark. "Mésange" is the name of the bird, like a small chickadee. K & G are the initials for Keller & Guérin. This set is half porcelain decorated with blue transfers of mésange birds and plants. It has unusual shapes with square angle handles and finials. $400-600.

    Teapot with cover 4.62" high,
    Creamer & covered sugar bowl,
    Three cups & three saucers 3.5" diameter.

"PORCELAINE OPAQUE, GIEN, FRANCE" is on the trademark. The company established a factory in 1864. Children's sets came from this factory at about the turn of the twentieth century. The transfers are blue with scenes from the story of Little Red Riding Hood. The French captions read, "Porte-lui cette galette," meaning bring her this tart. "Je vais voir gd maman," or I'm going to see Grandma.

    These pieces are half porcelain decorated with blue transfers. It is doll size. The tall creamer pictures Red Riding Hood and the teapot pictures a Wolf. *Courtesy of Isabelle Punchard.* $100-200.

    Round covered sugar bowl,
    Three cups and three saucers 2.75" diameter.

Left:
Portraits of Napoleon and Josephine adorn the porcelain cups. Napoleon Bonaparte (1769-1821) known as Napoleon I, was the French Emperor from 1804 to 1814. He married Josephine Tascher de La Pagerie in 1796. He divorced her in 1810 but still supported her until her death in 1814. The cups and saucers are decorated in maroon and green with gold trim. It would date in the first quarter of the twentieth century. It was questionable if this set should be included because the main pieces of this boxed set are nickel plated. They are marked "Excelsior - Nickel, P.S." The tray is 6 by 10.25 inches. $400-600.

    Teapot with cover 4.87" high,
    Creamer & covered sugar bowl,
    Compote and sugar tongs,
    Two cups & two saucers 3.5" diameter.

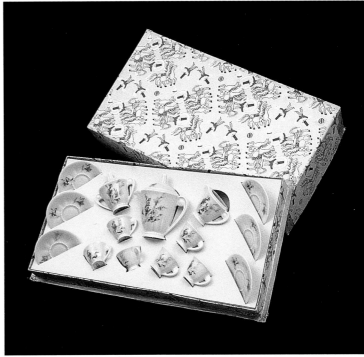

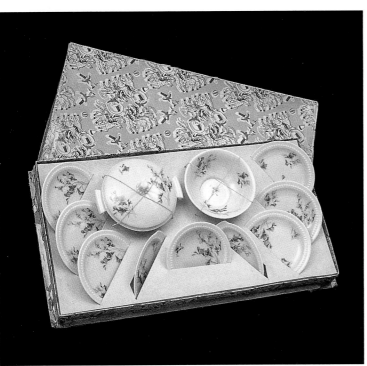

Above:
"FABRIQUE ROYALE LIMOGES, LIMOGES, FRANCE" is the information on the trademark. In 1784, when King Louis XVI bought the factory, the Royale name was used. When it was sold, the factory could continue using the Fabrique Royale name. The factory began in 1908 making miniatures and fancy porcelain. This set is typical of wares from around the 1920s. The glaze is buff color decorated with decals of flowers in red, yellow and blue. Fine craftsmanship compliments this toy set. The set came in its original cardboard box. $400-600.

    Teapot with cover 4.75" high,
    Creamer & covered sugar bowl,
    Six cups & six saucers 3.5" diameter.

A matching dinner set to the preceding tea set completes the services from the same company. It came in a matching cardboard box to the tea set. Keep in mind the European custom of serving tea or coffee after a meal. $400-600.

    Large covered serving dish 3.75" high,
    Four miscellaneous serving dishes,
    Six dinner plates 5.12" diameter.

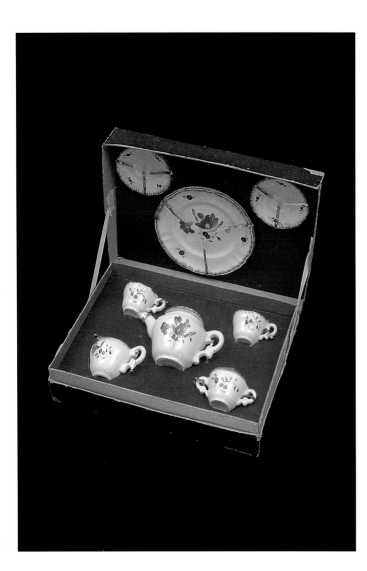

Left:
"LE JOUET, LONGCHAMP, J.L. ERMISSE" is printed on the cardboard box. This faience set would date circa 1930. It is decorated with feathered edges and hand painted flowers in red and blue with green leaves. $400-600.
    Teapot with cover 4.25" high,
    Creamer & covered sugar bowl,
    Large serving plate 6.37" diameter,
    Two cups & two saucers 3.5" diameter.

Below:
"PILIVITE, PORCELAINES Ë FEU, PILLIVUYT & CIE, MÉHUN, MADE IN FRANCE" is the information printed in gold letters. Charles Pillivuyt was a Swiss immigrant that started a French hard porcelain business in 1851. This type of mark was used between 1865 and 1948. This tea set dating 1930s to 1940s is decorated in the imitation of older patterns. In 1946 the company incorporated. It is fine porcelain decorated with a red outline, blue flowers and green leaves. The inside of the teapot has a porcelain guard to keep the tea leaves from plugging the holes to the spout. The cups are shaped like coffee mugs. $200-300.
    Teapot with cover 3.5" high,
    Covered sugar bowl,
    Four cups & four saucers 4.25" diameter.

PILIVITE
PORCELAINES
A FEU
PILLIVUYT & Cie
MEHUN
MADE IN FRANCE

Dinner Sets

Wonderful French porcelain and craftsmanship make this set special. It is of an exceptionally fine quality with artistic painting. The outline is black with hand painted blue leaves and orange flowers. Gold rims complete the decoration. It is a large beautiful set in both size and the number of pieces. *Courtesy of Isabelle Punchard.* $1800-2200.

Large covered tureen 4.87" high,
Two round covered dishes 3.5" high,
One sauce tureen 3.5" high,
One sauce boat, one compote,
Large open bowl,
Two platters 5.25 by 7.75" & 4.25 by 6.25 ",
Two oval dishes 3 by 5.37 inches,
One serving plate 5.25" diameter,
Six soup plates 4.87" diameter,
Twelve plates 4.87" diameter.

Most French porcelain toy dishes are beautiful. The porcelain is pure white and the decoration is hand painted. This set includes small colorful flowers, a pink band and gold trim. It includes thirty-four pieces in the dinner set, plus twenty pieces of glassware and pewter flatware for six place settings. *Courtesy of Isabelle Punchard.* $1800-2200.

    Tureen with cover, underplate 3.87" high,
    Oval sauce tureen with attached underplate 3" high,
    Fruit bowl with openwork 2.5" high,
    Butter or sauce boat with attached base,
    Two small covered serving dishes on small plates,
    Meat dishes 3.5 by 4.62 inches,
    Large open serving bowl,
    Tall compote 1.75" high, two short compotes,
    Two open serving dishes, two pickle dishes,
    Twelve plates for soup plates 3.12" diameter.

The glassware includes two decanters and three sizes of glasses, and they are:
    Decanters with stoppers are 8.25 and 6.5" high,
    Seven Champagne flutes 3.5" high,
    Six water glasses 3" high,
    Five wine glasses 2.25" high.

The soft pewter flatware includes six each knives (3.62" long), forks, and spoons. The front of the handles are plain with a pattern on the back side. To set the table, the decorations should be up with the fork tines turned down.

Above:
Early French porcelain sets often came unmarked. The porcelain is very white with hand painted brown tree stems, green leaves, and red berries or flowers circa 1880. The base of the tureen has a thick porcelain base typical of French wares. The sauce boat has an unusual shape, not like the usual French or German pieces. $700-900.

Tureen with cover & underplate 4.5" high,
Platter 3.75 by 5.37",
Covered & open serving dish,
Sauce boat, salt dip & compote,
Six soups & six plates all 3.25" diameter.

Left:
This doll-sized French dinner set has especially white porcelain. The hand painting of butterflies, bugs, toys, and flowers is excellent. Gold trim finishes decorating the set. It came packaged with old tissue in an oblong wicker box that may have been the original container. $700-900.

Tureen with cover 3.62" high,
Two platters 2.75 by 4.25",
Two serving dishes,
Two serving plates 3.87" diameter,
Five soup plates & five plates all 2.75" diameter.

Factories around Limoges produced fine porcelain dishes for children's play, circa 1900. This set also includes molding in the porcelain and gold trim. The unique decorations are the decals of people dressed in an Oriental style and single flowers that add interest. The ladies are dressed in Kimonos featuring seven different settings. $700-900.

    Tureen with cover 3.25" high, Covered serving dish,
    Sauce boat with attached base, Open serving bowl, two compotes,
    Platter, two relish dishes, Large shallow bowl & plate each 4.5" diameter,
    Six soup plates 3.5" diameter, Six plates 3.5" diameter.

"GIEN" is printed in the trademark circa 1890 to 1910. It is located near Orleans. The factory was established in 1864 to produce imitations of Italian Majolica styles. This dinner set is beautifully decorated in bright primary colors. The horn, flowers, and birds are an interesting combination. The cover has molded leaves colored green with black veins and a fruit bud for the finial. The rims and trim are dark blue. $700-900.

    Covered serving dish 3.62" high, Large open serving bowl, compote,
    Sauce boat, two relish dishes, platter, Large serving plate 5" diameter,
    Four soup plates & four dinner plates all 4.37" diameter, Two small plates 3.87" diameter.

French porcelain sets are very attractive and could usually withstand most play from children. The cobalt blue decorative scenes include waterfowl such as swans, ducks, and cranes in the water. Plants and flowers with gold accents and trim complete the setting. This partial set is heavy porcelain dating around the turn of the twentieth century. $400-600.

Large platter 4.25 by 5 inches, Small platter 2.5 by 3 inches,

Three section serving dish, Four tiny dishes with handles,

Two soup plates & five plates all 4" diameter, Six plates 2.87" diameter.

No trademark is given but the shape of the pieces, especially the sauce boat, is a French design circa 1880. It is a little larger than the preceding set. Each piece is decorated with hand painted red cherries, black stems, green and gold leaves and gold edge trim. *Courtesy of Diane Punchard.* $700-900.

Tureen with cover 3.75" high, Two platters 3.75 by 5.5 inches,

Small covered dish,

Large open bowl,

Two serving plates 4" diameter, Sauce boat & compote,

Two small open dishes, A double dish with a handle,

Six soups & six plates all 3.5" diameter.

Sarreguemines is a French factory and also the name of the town that appears quite often on children's items. Sarraguemines was started by Paul Utzschneider, circa 1770, in Lorraine, France. The mark is the company or town name. It could also have U.S. or U & C or U.S. in a triangle, or U & Cie in an octagon. This mark was used after 1890. The wares are usually cream colored with well placed decals. Sets may be a tea set or dinner set or toilet set, usually made in child play size rather than doll size. This dinner service set includes a border of continuous red flowers, and green stems and leaves. The decoration on the finials and handles has been hand painted. The extremely fine decals portray about twenty different scenes which include children, some adults, and animals in scenes or activities. This dinner service is the largest sized French set pictured. $1800-2200.

Two large covered serving dishes 5" high, One serving platter 5 by 7.5",
One square serving bowl, One sauce boat,
Five small plates 5.25" diameter, Eleven large plates 6.5" diameter.

"SERVICE, MÉNAGE" is on the top of the wooden box. Translated, it means everyday service. The box size is 11 1/2 by 16 1/2 by 5 inches high. It is covered with dark maroon paper to look like simulated leather. As it is opened, dishes fit into the cover and the front flap folds down to hold two pieces. The china trademark is "PORCELAIN OPAQUE DE GIEN" dating it about 1880 to 1910. The border on each piece is brown vine and leaves with some green leaves. The scenes on the dishes include children playing with the captions below the picture. The half porcelain dishes have brown transfers. Hand painting in red, green, yellow, blue, purple, gray, and brown are over the transfers.

"L'Hiver," meaning winter, shows three children making and throwing snow balls.

"Le Traineau," meaning sled, shows a boy pulling a girl on a sled, with a boy ice skating in the background.

"L'École Buissonnière" translates into playing hookey. Three children are shown picking flowers in an open field. Their books are on the ground.

"Le Collins-Maillard" shows three girls playing Blind Man's Buff.

"La Gourmandise," meaning sweet tooth, shows children eating. Besides the ceramic dishes, six glass pieces are included. They are two wine or water carafes, 4 inches high. Two goblets, 3 inches high, and two double dishes. Flatware for two place settings is included. Pink checkered napkins complete the set. $1000-1400.

 Round covered tureen 3.5" high,
 Two compotes, open deep bowl,
 Two small trays 3 by 5",
 Platter 3.5 by 5.5",
 One plate 5 " diameter,
 One plate & bowl both 4.25" diameter,
 Three plates 4" diameter.

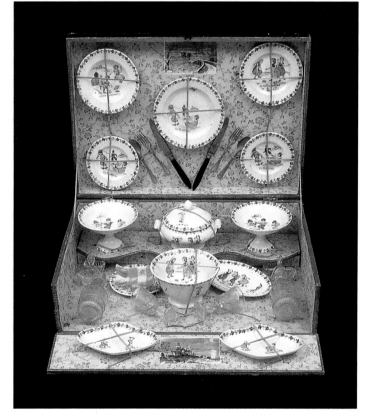

The second set with the same French trademark tells the story of Little Red Riding Hood. It has brown transfers with color hand painted over the glaze. This dinner set belonged to a little French girl, Andrée Albert, who was born in 1898 and received the dishes as a small child. It now belongs to her granddaughter, Isabelle. The French captions include "Ofl vas tu?" (Where are you going?); "Je vais voir gd maman" (I'm going to see Grandma); "Porte lui cette galette" (Take this pastry to her); "Prends ce chemin" (Take this trail); "Toc, toc" (Knock, knock); "Que vous avez de gdes oreilles" (You have such big ears). *Courtesy of Isabelle Punchard.* $700-900.

Tureen with cover 4.5" high,
Covered serving dish, open serving dish,
Sauce boat, two soup plates 4.37" diameter,
Eight plates 4.37" diameter.

Choisy LeRoi is credited as the maker of this dinner service set. The factory was founded by Clément in 1785. They started making hard paste porcelain then expanded their factories all through the 1800s. The main features are the round tureen and scalloped edges on all the pieces. It is half porcelain decorated with red transfers but it also came in other colors. It has a narrow stylized border with a seaside theme including transfers of ships, a lighthouse, a dock, people with fishing nets, sea gulls, an anchor, etc. $700-900.

Large tureen 5" high,
Covered serving bowl,
Platter 4.25 by 6.37",
Large open serving bowl,
Compote, two small dishes,
Large serving plate 5.5" diameter,
Five soup plates & nine plates 4" diameter,
Five small plates 3" diameter.

"OPAQUE, LUNÉVILLE" is on the trademark. The makers are Keller & Guérin, located in Lunéville, circa 1880s. All the pieces are hand painted. The main color on the border, finials, and in the flowers is deep pink. The stems are black with green leaves and touches of yellow, purple, and blue in the flowers. The covers and platters have a green bug painted on them. $700-900.

Large covered tureen 3.75" high,
Two round covered serving dishes 2.75" high,
Small tureen with attached base,
Deep open serving bowl,
Two compotes 3.5" diameter,
Sauce boat with attached base,
Small open serving dish 2 by 4 inches,
Two platters 4 by 6.25 inches,
Serving plate 4.5" diameter,
Six soups & four plates all 4" diameter.

"K & G, LUNÉVILLE" is on the trademark of this French dinner service. K & G are the initials for Keller & Guérin. It is decorated with brown transfers of fun whimsical scenes for children. Some scenes include a small boy with a large hat and large pipe; two boys carrying a large fish; a lobster biting a boy; a boy pulling a wagon; a dog pulling a wagon; a goose pulling on a girl's dress; and different animals in various scenes. $700-900.

K & G
LUNÉVILLE

  Small tureen with cover 4.12" high,
  Large covered serving dish, Large open dish,
  Sauce boat, two compotes, Six large plates 5.5" diameter.

"ST. AMAND ET HAMAGE (NORD)" is the printed trademark information. The company is in Saint-Amand-les-Eaux in the North of France. This faience (earthenware) dinner set, circa 1900 is decorated with transfers in green color. They include children with animals and at play or work. The border is a small repeat design. $700-900.

ST AMAND
et
(NORD)
HAMAGE

  Large tureen with cover 5" high, Two covered serving dishes,
  Two large open serving bowls 5.25" top diameter, Two compotes, two relish dishes,
  Three meat platters, sauce boat, Large serving plate 5.37" diameter,
  Eight soup plates 4" diameter, Ten dinner plates 4" diameter,
  Seven smaller plates 3.37" diameter.

"S C" is the mark for the Société de la Rue Chaptal in Paris. In 1862 Savarin, a clockmaker, invented a machine to paint on porcelain. This company was an association of amateur decorators. The SC mark is on the three largest pieces and the number 31 is on all the pieces. This would be the decorator's number, dating after 1880. The material is half porcelain glazed, with all the flower decorations hand painted. Every piece is painted with a black outline, green and yellow leaves, pink and blue flowers with yellow centers. The border and finial trim are deep royal blue. $700-900.

    Large covered tureen 3.25" high,
    Large round covered serving dish,
    Large open serving bowl,
    Small covered sauce tureen with attached base,
    Sauce pitcher with attached base,
    Two compotes of different heights,
    Large platter 4 by 6.25",
    Small open serving dish,
    Serving plate 4.75" diameter,
    Eight soups & eight plates all 4" diameter.

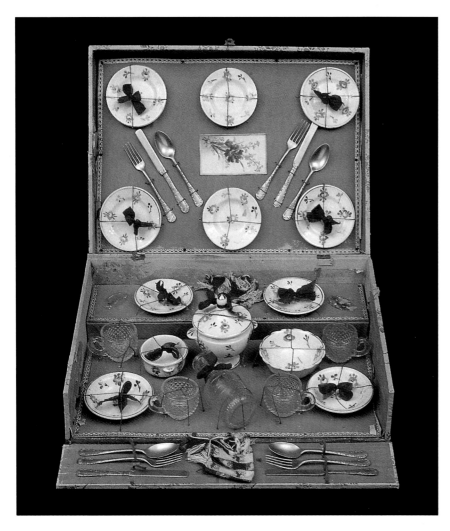

"SERVICE de TABLE, PARIS" is printed on the cover of the wooden box. It would date around the turn of the twentieth century up to 1914. The set includes the china, glassware, nickel silver flatware and napkins, everything a child would need to serve a meal. The china is half porcelain, decorated with hand painted pink flowers and green leaves with gold trim. $600-800.

    Tureen with cover 3.5" high,
    Two serving pieces,
    Four soups & four plates all 3" diameter,
    Four glass cups & carafe,
    Four knives, forks, & spoons,
    Four red checkered napkins.

Quimper is a French term for faience (earthenware) manufactured near Quimper, France, that began in 1690. The modern marks "HENRIOT" or "H.B" have been used since 1872. "FRANCE" on the trademark would date it after 1891. Quimper ware is still being produced.

The two tiny plates and one larger plate at the top are hand painted designs dating between 1872 and 1891. The other four pieces would date after 1891. All the pieces are hand painted. The two larger Quimper plates are pottery decorated with Breton peasants in their traditional garb. The typical folk art figures are painted in bright primary colors with blue rims. Each piece $50-100.

    Tiny plate 2.12" diameter,
    Small plate 3" diameter,
    Two plates 4" diameter,
    Platter 4.25 by 6",
    Covered serving dish.

This small-sized dinner set is Quimper decorated with the same hand painted Breton peasants in primary colors. The set is not trademarked but would date after 1891. The pieces picture a man or a woman with blue and yellow bands. The tureen cover does not have a cutout for the handle of the ladle. $800-1200.

    Tureen with cover 3 " high,
    Serving platter 2.87 by 4.37",
    Sauce pitcher, small serving bowl,
    Serving plate 4.37" diameter,
    Four soup plates 3.12" diameter,
    Four plates 3.12" diameter.

"ROSE ROUGE, H B C M, FRANCE, DECOR A LA MAIN" is printed in the trademark. Rose Rouge means Red Rose. Décor Ë La Main means hand decorated, most likely from the 1920s or 1930s. This half porcelain set has hand painted red roses and blue trim under the glaze. This same basic mold has been decorated with rabbits and most likely other decorations. $700-900.

Covered serving dish 3.75" high,
Large open serving dish,
Large serving plate 5.25" diameter,
One platter 4 by 5.75",
One tray with handles 3.25 by 7.25",
Two little dishes & cream pitcher,
Six soups & six plates all 4.25" diameter,
Six cups & six saucers 3.25" diameter.

French faience is also called soft-paste, half-porcelain, pottery or earthenware. This dinner set has a cream color base decorated with stencils. The checkered design is red. The individual pieces include one to three bunnies outlined in black in each scene. It would date around the 1920s. $600-800.

Large tureen with cover 5" high,
Covered serving dish 3.75" high,
Large open bowl 5.25" diameter,
Compote, sauce boat, small serving piece,
Two platters 5 by 7.25" & 4.5 by 6.5",
Three large serving plates 5.5 to 6",
Six soup plates & six plates all 4.87" diameter.

This French faience dinner set is creamy colored, decorated with stencils in green and red. The design of the stencils shows a stylized type of flower that was especially popular about the 1920s. There is no cutout in the tureen cover. $600-800.

Large covered tureen 5" high,
Two covered serving dishes 3.75" high,
Open serving bowl, shallow bowl, small serving piece,
Platter 4.5 by 6.5",
Large plate 5.5" diameter,
Four plates 4.75" diameter,
Four cups & four saucers 3.25" diameter,
Six soup plates 4.87" diameter,
Six plates 4.87" diameter.

Another French faience dinner set is similar to the preceding set. The handles are styled the same but it has a little change in the design. The stencils are blue cats with yellow flowers on the borders. $600-800.
    Large covered serving bowl,
    Smaller covered serving bowl,
    Open bowl, compote,
    Sauce boat with attached underplate,
    Eight plates 5" diameter,
    Four cups & four saucers 3.25" diameter.

"FT, TOKIO, BADONVILLER" is printed on the trademark. This is a mid-twentieth century set. It is not very good quality earthenware. The set is decorated with decals in an oriental theme called "TOKIO." The decals include pagodas, a bridge, two people in a boat and foliage with orange rims. $200-300.
    Covered serving dish,
    Two compotes 4.25" diameter,
    Large open bowl, serving dish,
    Large plate 4.75" diameter,
    Three small plates 3.37" diameter.

"LA DINETTE de MICKEY MOUSE" is printed on the inside of the cardboard box cover. La Dinette means the dining set. The china is trademarked "LICENCE WALT DISNEY, SINGER, LIMOGES." The company Singer began in 1950. It is decorated with Walt Disney decals and pink line trim. The characters include Minnie Mouse; Donald Duck; Huey, Dewey, & Louie Duck; Three dwarfs Doc, Bashful and Grumpy; Geppetto; Joe Carioca; Jiminy Cricket; Big Bad Wolf; and Bambi. $500-700.
    Covered serving dish 2.37" high,
    Five miscellaneous serving dishes,
    Six plates 3" diameter.

La Dinette
de
Mickey Mouse

Miscellaneous

"Chocolate" from France was prepared by simmering cocoa with a little water on the stove, then serving it in the pot, and pouring it into cups where cream or milk and sugar were added at the table. That is why the creamer and sugar bowl are large compared to the serving pot. This chocolate pot is porcelain with a side handle. The cups are tall. It is decorated with delicate flowers. $1000-1200.

   Chocolate pot with cover 5.5" high,
   Cream or milk pitcher, open sugar bowl,
   Four cups and four saucers 3.25" diameter.

Right:
Veilleuse is a French term pronounced "Va Use." It is a ceramic utensil for keeping a teapot, bowl, or cup warm. The hollow pedestal stand has an opening for a godet (the lamp). The characteristic feature on the teapot is the projecting bottom which fits into the pedestal. This way, the bottom of the pot is closer to the heat source to keep the tea warm. This French veilleuse has hand painted flowers with heavy gold trim. It has very white porcelain with a thick base. The hand painted initials "V.P." are for the decorator but no manufacturer's trademark is given. The round holes around the top are for air so the candle will stay lit. The whole unit is 5.5 inches high. $150-250.

Left:
Food warming dishes had a space for hot water to keep the food warm. These are twentieth century pieces. This toy example is marked "Made In France, Limoges." The dress of the children would date around the 1930s to 1940s. The hole for hot water is plugged with a cork. The little boy and girl are wearing shorts and a top with matching shoes. They are surprised by a duck. The warming plate is 3.5 inches in diameter. $75-125.

Dresser sets are quite unique. This French porcelain is pure white with heavy base rims. It is decorated with pink bands, little hand painted flowers with green leaves and gold trim. $300-500.
  Dresser tray 3 by 6",
  Two tall covered jars 4.12" high,
  Covered powder jar 1.5" high.

OILETTE" was the only marking on the box of this French shstand set. The individual pieces are not marked. The pieces earthenware decorated with a blue floral transfer pattern. 0-500.
Water pitcher 5.5" high,
Wash bowl 7.5" diameter,
Oblong covered dish 2.25 by 5 inches,
Hair receiver dish 3.5" wide,
Covered powder dish 3.5" wide.

Trademarks on pottery and porcelain are important for identifying the country of origin, manufacturer, and date. The factories in this area are some of the most productive in Europe. This map identifies areas such as Bavaria as well as factory locations. The two World Wars in this century have destroyed many factories and records. With so many locations, this map gives a sense of the importance of this trade.

Germany

Tea Pot, Coffee Pot, Chocolate or Cocoa Pot

Germany exported large quantities of children's play dishes from the 1870s to the First World War in 1914. Prior to this time there were limited numbers of dishes from some of the finest companies. Meissen produced a flower encrusted set that was for sale in 1993 priced at eight thousand dollars. Today they are museum pieces. After World War I ended in 1918 the factories began rebuilding. Some sets that are trademarked but do not have "Made In Germany" were not intended for export. Many of the earlier sets were not marked at all, and later were usually marked "Germany" or "Made In Germany." Since 1891 the McKinley Tariff Act required that all items imported into the United States have "Made In" country of origin. A few sets included the manufacturer's trademark. Sometimes only one piece in a set was marked.

The German occupation held by the American, English, and French created the Federal Republic of Germany on September 21, 1949. In 1952 the German Democratic Repub-

lic (East) announced measures to isolate from the Federal Republic of Germany (West). Americans refer to them as East Germany and West Germany. The Berlin Wall began in August 1961 and was torn down in 1989. Dishes or toys marked Federal Republic of Germany (West) would date between 1949 and 1989. Dishes marked German Democratic Republic (East) would date 1952 to 1989.

A majority of the German dishes are porcelain, ranging from very fine to poor quality. The best dishes could include molded in relief, fancy handles and finials with beading and embossed scrolls, perfectly placed decals, and quality craftsmanship. The other range is earthenware, poor quality work with flaws and bumps, crooked decals, and uneven shapes using unskilled labor.

Favorite topics for decorating play dishes include scenes of children at play, faces of children, scenes from nursery rhymes, and pictures of various animals. German makers often used gold trim or luster in their decorating. Pink luster was the most commonly used color. Lusters in blue to blue-gray to gray-green were also used, as were yellow and mother-of-pearl.

Some manufacturers produced undecorated white china that was either sold for use as white ware or sold to other companies to be decorated. Decals were made and sold to any company. That is the reason you can find the same decals on dishes from different manufacturers and countries. Consequently, the collector today may find a confusing mixture: that is, the same decals may appear on differing china shapes. This casual inconsistency was acceptable because the dishes were intended solely as playthings.

German tea or coffee sets have a basic unit of a server with a cover, cream pitcher, and a sugar bowl either covered or open. A few German sets have an extra bowl that is close in size to the sugar bowl, which may have been intended for sugar lumps. Other pieces may include two cups and saucers and maybe two plates, or one serving dish or a tray.

Another combination is four cups and saucers with or without plates. A large set would include six cups and saucers with or without plates or possibly with one or two serving dishes. German dinner sets were manufactured in sizes ranging from small dollhouse size to a large size for little girls to actually have a meal. A dinner service would generally include about twelve to twenty-five pieces.

Children's sets were patterned after adult services including tea sets, coffee sets, chocolate sets, dinner service sets, toilet sets, and miscellaneous specialty sets. Germany served more coffee than tea so it stands to reason that more coffee services were made for children. When little girls had a party it would usually be referred to as a tea party regardless of what beverage was being served.

At the end of each description the pieces included in the set will be listed. Keep in mind the same serving pieces could include a service for two, four or six place settings

German Tea Sets

Meissen was the first German porcelain factory which began in 1710 by Royal decree. Porcelain was perfected by Friedrich Wilhelm Bottger. The factory was located at Dresden as were at least thirty other factories, many of which imitated the style of Meissen or a version of their mark to confuse the buyer. Meissen has used a version of the crossed sword trademark since 1724. This blue underglaze hand painted trademark would date between 1814 and 1860.
Sprigging is the process of attaching small individual pieces to form flowers and leaves. They are applied with slip (liquid clay), then glazed and fired. It is also referred to as applied or encrusted flowers.
This Meissen partial set has applied flowers on the teapot, the outside of the cup, and underside of the saucer. Small hand painted flowers are on the inside bottom of the cup and the center of the saucer. A small hand painted bug and butterfly add decoration to the teapot. Three small moths are hand painted around the flowers on the saucer. The teapot is 2.75 inches high with a replaced cover. The cup and saucer have the number 27 which is the decorator's number. The saucer is 2.75 inches in diameter. $700-900.

Sitzendorf in Thuringer, Germany, began a porcelain factory in 1850 in the imitation of Meissen porcelains with encrusted flowers. Encrusted flowers are a real work of art and may be called sprigging. Clay flowers and leaves were molded or stamped separately, then attached to the object with slip before firing. With this process the designs were precolored and held their color when fired. All the pieces in this set are heavily decorated with beautifully encrusted colorful flowers and veined leaves. The finials are a rose. Little bugs and butterflies are painted around the encrusted flowers and inside the cups. The saucers have hand painted flowers on the top side and encrusted flowers on the bottom side. The creamer is round while the teapot and sugar bowl are square shaped, but the flowers and bugs are of the same type and coloring on all the pieces. The work is exquisite and could be considered a cabinet piece. $900-1200.

Teapot with cover 3.5" high,
Creamer & covered sugar bowl,
Two cups & two saucers 2.75" diameter.

Notice this exceptionally fine, molded in relief, pure white porcelain set. The bottom of the serving pieces and cup have added reinforcement porcelain bars for strength. The decoration includes hand applied gold trim on the relief decoration and handles, gold line trim and a gold wash on the inside of the cup. There is no trademark on the pieces but because of the quality it should date after 1870. Adult sets were made in this same style. This set could have been intended as an individual service rather than a toy. $400-600.

Teapot with cover 4.5" high,
Creamer & covered sugar bowl,
One cup & one saucer 4" diameter.

German porcelain sets were made in all sizes at reasonable prices for children's or doll's parties. This set would serve the little girl and her larger doll. It is trimmed in cobalt blue luster with gold flowers dating about 1870 to 1880s. There is nice embossing on the teapot spout. On less expensive wares, it was common to decorate the front and leave the back plain. *Courtesy of Flora Jane Steffen.* $400-600.

Teapot with cover 5.37" high,
Creamer & sugar bowl,
Two cups & two saucers 3.25" diameter.

This set came decorated with a blue band and gold trim as well as all white with gold trim. These German porcelain tea services are beautifully molded and date around the 1870s. The shapes are of an earlier style with a tall creamer which includes a wide lip. The sugar bowl is bulbous with two small side handles. The serving pot is not tall and includes a high spout like that of the coffee server. The cups are tea-cup shaped. Blue band set *courtesy of Isabelle Punchard.* Each set $500-700.

    Teapot with cover 5" high,
    Creamer & covered sugar bowl,
    Six plates 4" diameter,
    Six cups & six saucers 4" diameter.

Germany manufactured some unique sets. This set includes cherubs as finials and handles, plus two cherubs beside the teapot spout. The faces are nicely painted by an artist. The porcelain set is well crafted. A cherub is without clothes as an innocent child, whereas an angel wears clothes. On a slip of paper inside the teapot someone had written "Aunt Lucy Gardner's doll's tea set 1875." $700-900.

    Teapot with cover 5.25" high,

    Creamer & covered sugar bowl,

    Four cups & four saucers 3.75" diameter.

Notice the delicate designs of the serving pieces. It is a nicely made porcelain tea set with pink bands outlined in gold. The shape of the serving pieces are of an earlier design, circa 1870s. The creamer is tall with a wide lip. The teapot has a recessed cover, nice molding on the base of the spout, and a fancy moulded handle. $400-600.

    Teapot with cover 4.5" high,

    Creamer & covered sugar bowl,

    Four plates 4.75" diameter,

    Four cups & four saucers 4.25" diameter.

A plain white small porcelain tea set is not trademarked but the shapes should date this set about 1870-1880. The teapot cover is recessed, the handle is a high loop. The cream pitcher is tall with a fairly wide lip and high handle. The sugar bowl is large with the cover fitting over the top rim. The cups and saucers are plain. $100-200.

    Teapot with cover 4" high,
    Creamer & covered sugar bowl,
    Four cups & four saucers 3.87" diameter.

German factories produced some small-sized tea sets with lovely shapes. It would date about 1880-1890. The trim is a simple red line design with gold trim. The teapot cover is recessed, the creamer has a wide lip. The set has an elegant style. $100-200.

    Teapot with cover 4.5" high,
    Creamer & covered sugar bowl,
    Six cups & six saucers 3.5" diameter.

Small doll-sized tea sets came in all white, with no trim other than embossed decoration. This one would date late eighteenth century and would fit perfectly with a table setting of German dolls. Just study the shapes in the picture and appreciate the maker. $100-200.

    Teapot with cover 3.12" high,
    Creamer & covered sugar bowl,
    Five cups & five saucers 2.62" diameter.

Early German dishes came packaged in wooden boxes. The box size is 7 by 8 inches by 3 inches high. There is a black & white picture of a tea set on the cover of the box. The same white porcelain tea set with aqua bands and gold trim is in the box. On the bottom of the wooden box is written in pencil "Elizabeth Dufoyr, June 17, 1877, From Father." *Courtesy of Helga Stuewer.* $300-500.

Teapot with cover 3" high,
Creamer & covered sugar bowl,
Six cups & six saucers 2.87" diameter.

This fine porcelain tea set is doll-size, decorated in a style from the Meissen factory. It has deep blue flowers, a version of the straw flower. German manufacturers produced numerous molds using this basic pattern with variations. *Courtesy of Flora Jane Steffen.* $400-600.

Teapot with cover 2.62" high,
Creamer & sugar bowl,
Five cups & five saucers 2.25" diameter.

67

German porcelain dishes are still being found with notable characteristics. This is the first set pictured with handles molded in the form of a cable or rope pattern. The raised cord and tassel decoration carry out this theme. The decorative cord looks as if it had been pulled tight, giving the porcelain a crimped look. This crimping is also at the base of the serving pieces, the cups, and on the plates. These shapes could also be called Victorian Baroque, dated after 1870. The decals include several shades of blue Forget-Me-Not flowers. $400-600.

Teapot with cover 5.25" high, Creamer & covered sugar bowl,
Six plates 4.25" diameter, Six cups & six saucers 3.75" diameter.

This trademark is from the Tiefenfurt factory in Schlesien Germany. They began making porcelain wares in 1883. This is a brightly colored tea set of deep pink and light green on the square corners. This unique mold has crimping on all the pieces. The color and style look more like a French design. The handles, trim, and edges are all painted gold. This fine porcelain set is delicate and would not stand abuse from children. $400-600.

Teapot with cover 4.5" high, Creamer & covered sugar bowl,
Four plates 4.25" diameter, Four cups & four saucers 3" diameter.

German porcelain tea sets included some unique shapes. The early features include the tall cream pitcher with the wide lip. There is gold trim on the teapot spout and where each handle is attached. The rims, handles, and tip of the finials are orange. It is a finely crafted set circa 1880s. $200-300.

　　Teapot with cover 5.25" high,
　　Creamer & covered sugar bowl,
　　Six cups & six saucers 4" diameter.

Some factory in Germany made this fine unmarked tea set that is still packaged in the original wooden box, circa 1880s. Covers for the teapot and sugar bowl are like a "mushroom cap" and the creamer has a wide lip. The background is light green with decals of colorful figures and hand painted purple flowers and dark green leaves. The decals include a little girl in a purple dress and hat sitting reading a book with a dog sitting by her side; a girl in an orange dress and hat riding her bicycle; a boy in a blue sailor-type suit riding a bicycle with his hat flying off; a boy in a brown sailor-type suit holding a stick; a girl in an orange dress and hat waving; and a man in a blue suit with knickers playing golf. The six saucers just have the painted flowers. $500-700.

　　Teapot with cover 3.5" high,
　　Creamer & covered sugar bowl,
　　Six plates 3.75" diameter,
　　Six cups & six saucers 3.25" diameter.

R. S. Prussia china was made by a member of the Schlegelmilch family who came from the town of Sulh, Thuringia, Germany. Prussia was a state in Germany. R. S. stood for Rudolph Schlegelmilch, in honor of the father of Erdmann and Reinhold. Erdmann Schlegelmilch established a factory in Sulh in 1861. A younger brother, Reinhold, worked for his brother before moving to Tillowitz in 1869, where he opened a factory. A nephew, Oscar, located his factory in Langewiesen in 1892. The wares included numerous different marks in various colors, or as is the case of most toy dishes, they are found unmarked. Because they all used similar patterns, designs, and finishes, it is extremely difficult to determine the exact factory or location where these children's play sets were manufactured. There are eight sets from R.S. Prussia pictured in this series. The dates would be between 1869 and 1910.

This R. S. Prussia child's unmarked coffee set is fine porcelain molded in relief. The relief on the edges are floral patterns that remain white with some gold trim. Next to that, pieces are shaded blue at the edges fading to white. The center decoration includes scenic views of either a castle or cottage with trees and greenery. Serving pieces and plates include two swallows, the saucers each have one swallow, and the cups include four swallows each. The swallows look as if they were a transfer for the breast and beak, with the wings and tail being hand painted. The finials are a pointed floral design. The handles are ornate and very graceful. All the pieces are beautifully crafted, which makes an appealing set. $2500-3000.
    Coffeepot with cover 6.25" high,
    Creamer & covered sugar bowl,
    Four plates 6" diameter,
    Four cups & four saucers 4.25" diameter.

R. S. Prussia produced this fine set in cobalt blue decorated with a decal of a cherub on the teapot and flowers on the creamer and sugar bowl. All pieces include small gold flowers and gold trim. The plates, cups and saucers are all cobalt. The history to date this set is that Betty Sweet Weyel's grandfather gave her this set when she was a small child, she was born in 1896 so the set would date early 1900s. $1300-1700.

    Teapot with cover 4.25" high,
    Creamer & covered sugar bowl,
    Six plates 2.75" diameter,
    Six cups & six saucers 2.75" diameter.

This R. S. Prussia tea set has the same mold as the preceding set. It came in the original box with no marking on the box or on the dishes. The decal is a scene of a windmill by the water and trees in the background. $1000-1200.

    Teapot with cover 4.25" high,
    Creamer & covered sugar bowl,
    Six plates 2.75" diameter,
    Six cups & six saucers 2.75" diameter.

This is a popular mold for R. S. Prussia toy tea sets. They were decorated with numerous designs and colors. Each piece is molded with small flowers and scrolling on the outside. A row of beading is at the base of the serving pieces. The handles and teapot spout are molded with the pieces and not applied afterward.

One set is decorated with swans on a lake with tall evergreens in the background. The china background is shaded blue. The swan set came in the original box including two serving plates, the other sets each have one serving plate. There are many more sets in this mold decorated differently. Each set $900-1400.

One set has a scenic scene with a house, cattle and a man.

One set is decorated with blue luster, gold trim, and soft flowers in pink to rose.

    Teapot with cover 5" high,
    Creamer & covered sugar bowl,
    Serving plate 5.5" diameter, to outside handles.
    Six cups & six saucers 3.75" diameter.

R. S. Prussia produced this tea set with an entirely different mold but the same style finial. It is beautifully crafted. The serving pieces are footed with four little feet. It is shaded with pink, and a brighter red than is usual on R. S. Prussia. Gold trim finishes the decoration. $800-1000.

Teapot with cover 4.25" high, Creamer & covered sugar bowl, Six cups & six saucers 2.87" diameter.

A soft delicate tea set is another style from R. S. Prussia. The main characteristics of R. S. Prussia are finely detailed molds. The porcelain is thin and one can feel the molded shapes on the inside of the serving pieces. All the sets have high quality control with the company using skilled labor. Small soft flowers, gold trim and rims with peach color panels decorate this set. *Courtesy of Diane Punchard.* $800-1000.

Teapot with cover 4" high,
Creamer & covered sugar bowl,
Six cups & six saucers 4" diameter.

Right:
A look of flow blue defines this German porcelain tea set. It is a blue spatter with gold gilding hand painted in a freehand design. There is no manufacturer's trademark but it does include a guilder's mark. $300-400.

Teapot with cover 3.25" high,
Cream pitcher,
Four plates 4.75" diameter,
Four small cups & four saucers 3" diameter.

This lovely tea set is of fine quality porcelain with scalloped edges, circa 1900. It has a stylized blue pattern with gold trim. The sugar bowl is the same size as the teapot and would be for coarse sugar, not like the refined sugar we now have. The creamer is small. $300-400.

 Teapot with cover 3.87" high,
 Creamer & large covered sugar bowl,
 Two cups & two saucers 4.5" diameter.

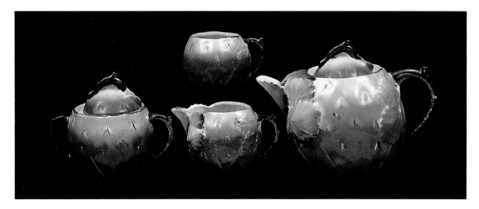

Strawberry is the theme of this porcelain tea set. The only mark is a mold number. Royal Bayreuth made some novelty sets but this is not as fine as their wares. Each piece represents a large strawberry with green leaves and brown twig handles and finials. Other fruits and vegetables are models for tea sets. $300-400.

 Teapot with cover 4.25" high,
 Creamer & covered sugar bowl,
 Two cups.

A German porcelain factory produced this fine quality play tea set. It is decorated to look like green leaves over a pine cone or nut center. The colors are unusual, the green leaves fading to teal with peach color edges and brown outlines. The handle and spout represent branches. The shapes are unique, carrying the same theme on all the pieces. Coloring and quality could attribute this set to Royal Bayreuth. *Courtesy of Flora Jane Steffen.* $400-600.

 Teapot with cover 4.5" high,
 Creamer & covered sugar bowl,
 Six cups & six saucers 4" diameter.

"Alice In Wonderland" is the children's classic written by Charles Lutwidge Dodgson, who used the pen name Lewis Carroll. He loved children and in 1862, told a story to a little girl, Alice Lidell, which he called "Alice's Adventures Underground." In 1865, the story was published as "Alice In Wonderland." Characters on the tea set are exact copies from the original engravings by John Tenniel. This set came from England with the Rd. No. 446137 dating this set 1904. The background color is green. The porcelain is German, and was probably made as a special order for a company in England. Characters include Alice at the tea party, the Duchess, Tweedledum, Tweedledee, the Mad Hatter, March Hare, and Dormouse. $400-600.

    Teapot with cover 3.5" high,
    Creamer & covered sugar bowl,
    Four cups & four saucers 3.75" diameter.

The information on these pieces is "Entered at Stationers Hall." It is German porcelain made for the English market with captions written in English. It is a nice porcelain with the same mold as the "Alice In Wonderland" tea set. The decals are Chinese children with long pig-tails. The caption on the teapot is "You know of course, a pig-tail does to draw a horse." The sugar bowl has a child sitting on a dock reading a book with his pig-tail to the water with the caption "While studying his lesson book, he fishes with his pig-tail hook." The cup caption is "Sometimes a teasing Chinese Boy, His fellow playmates will annoy." This set would date in the early 1900s. Nearly one hundred years later, I hope no one is offended by the captions. $400-600.

    Teapot with cover 3.5" high,
    Covered sugar bowl,
    One cup & one saucer 3.75" diameter.

BAVARIA

Royal Bayreuth of Bavaria is the oldest privately managed porcelain factory. The factory at Tettau, West Germany, was established in 1792 and is still in business despite many changes. The children's wares would date mostly between 1890 and 1914. This factory produced fine quality dinnerware, tapestry, decorative pieces, and many novelty items. Even the items that were unique in design were exceptionally well decorated. Royal Bayreuth made wares to be exported to America which usually displayed the blue trademark or no mark. Most of the novelty items were made before 1917 when Royal Bayreuth had a large fire that destroyed almost all the molds. This is one company that used a blue trademark on wares shipped to America while the wares with green trademarks were intended for Great Britain. Some of the children's scenes include Sunbonnet Babies, Snow Babies, Beach Babies, Ring-Around-The-Rosie, Little Bo Peep, Girl and Dog, and Nursery Rhymes.

"The Sunbonnet Babies' Party."

Here we are at the party.
Three little girls and three little
  dolls.
It is a Sunbonnet Babies' party.
See what good things we have
  to eat.
Don't you wish you had some?
We cannot give you any.
It is all for us.
This is our party.

Bertha L. Corbett Melchner was the creator of Molly and May, better known as Sunbonnet Babies. She could show character and feeling without showing a face. The Sunbonnet Babies were popular during the 1890s and into the 1920s. *The Sunbonnet Babies Book,* written by Eulalie Osgood Grover and illustrated by Bertha Corbett Melchner, was published in 1902.

The scenes are Sunday, fishing; Monday, washing; Tuesday, ironing; Wednesday, mending; Thursday, scrubbing; Friday, sweeping; Saturday, baking. These scenes were all applied on a set of seven porcelain plates produced by Royal Bayreuth, Bavaria, Germany. Children's toy coffee and cocoa sets have also been made with the Sunbonnet Babies decor. Most of these are unmarked, but are fine quality sets. $1300-1700.

Teapot with cover 3.25" high, To the top of the handle 4.5",
Creamer & covered sugar bowl, Two plates 4.5" diameter,
Two cups & two saucers 4" diameter.

These two sets of Beach Babies and Snow Babies have the same mold as the preceding Sunbonnet Babies set. They are unmarked but have the quality of Royal Bayreuth. The features include evenly placed decals, bright colors, and well-defined background scenes with details showing sand, sea, snow, grass, and sky. These sets were popular in the early 1900s. The teapots are all the same shape and size, but the rest of the pieces came in a larger or small scale. These sets were packaged with two, four, or six place settings with or without tea plates. Each set $400-600.
Sizes are the same as the previous set.

This set and the next two sets have the quality and coloring of Royal Bayreuth. They did a fine job of matching background colors with the decals. Scenes include a girl herding three geese; a woman gathering grain with two chickens near her; a man working in the field with three chickens in the background; a man standing and watching two turkeys; a man standing between two donkeys; a man sitting on a log near his two donkeys. The people, birds, and trees are decals. The rest of the decoration has been hand painted. The bottom half colors range from yellow to orange with a gray horizon. A little green grass and very soft clouds add up to a very attractive set. The handles are painted gold as are the rims on all the pieces. $400-600.

    Teapot with cover 3.75" high,
    Creamer & covered sugar bowl,
    Serving plate 5.5" diameter,
    Two plates 4.25" diameter,
    Two cups & two saucers 4" diameter.

Royal Bayreuth is being credited for this set. The shapes are the same as the preceding set. The bottom half of these pieces are brown shaded to look like a floor. The top half is tan with a shaded window. One decal includes a fat little boy blowing a horn and pulling a train by a string. The other decal is a fat little girl pushing her doll buggy.

This set includes serving pieces and two place settings, same size as the preceding set. $300-400.

Another set is pictured with the same shape as the two preceding sets. Serving pieces are a little larger, but the cups and saucers are the same size. The coloring has been beautifully painted with green grass, a horizon background, and a sky with light clouds. Three different colorful decals include four girls playing ring-around-the-rosie; two girls on a teeter-totter with a third girl watching a small dog; and the third scene is three little girls and a big dog with one small girl sitting on the dog's back. $400-600.

    Teapot with cover 4.25" high,
    Cream pitcher,
    Six cups & six saucers 4" diameter.

Brownies were created by Palmer Cox (1840 to 1924). They are versions of elfin-like creatures from the folklore legends of Scotland told to him by his Scottish grandmother. Mr. Cox said "Brownies, like fairies, were imaginary little sprites who were supposed to delight in harmless pranks while weary households slept, and never allowed themselves to be seen by mortals." The first Brownie drawings and stories appeared in the *St. Nicholas* magazine in 1883. *The Brownies, Their Book* was published in 1887. Palmer Cox copyrighted and patented twelve Brownie figures in 1892, and these figures were applied on many items. In 1895 the Brownie craze extended into children's tea sets. This set includes scenes of Brownies in action and would date about the turn of the twentieth century. $1000-1400.

    Teapot with cover 4.5" high,
    Creamer & covered sugar bowl,
    Six plates 3.25" diameter,
    Six cups & six saucers 2.75" diameter.

Rose Cecil O'Neill (1874-1944) was a naturally gifted person. She was a self taught artist and the creator of the famous "Kewpies" who first appeared in 1909. She said Kewpies, elf-like creatures, came to her in a dream. She loved children and brought out their characteristics in Kewpies. The top knot was that little wisp of hair that stands up on the pillow after a baby has been asleep. Children's play dishes, with the Kewpie decals, were made by Royal Rudolstadt in Prussia, and companies in Germany, Bavaria and Czechoslovakia. Kewpie items have been produced in Germany since 1913. This set is signed "Rose O'Neill, Kewpie, Germany." This fine German porcelain set dates circa 1915. It is a nice white porcelain with pink luster and at least two Kewpies on each piece, except the saucers. $1000-1400.

COPYRIGHTED
Rose O'Neill Wilson
KEWPIE
GERMANY

Rose o'neill
Kewpie
Germany

   Teapot with cover 5.5" high,
   Creamer & covered sugar bowl,
   Six plates 5.25" diameter,
   Six cups & six saucers 4.5" diameter.

   "Copyrighted, Mrs. Rose O'Neill Wilson, Kewpies, Bavaria" is the back stamp on this Kewpie set. White porcelain is decorated with gold trim, and two or more Kewpie decals on each piece. $1000-1400.

Copyrighted
Mrs. Rose O'Neill Wilson
Kewpies

BAVARIA

   Teapot with cover 4.75" high,
   Creamer & covered sugar bowl,
   Four cups & four saucers 4.25" diameter.

Rose O'Neill's Kewpie dishes were sold in several sizes. This is a small size that would be just perfect to use in a table setting with dolls. There is one Kewpie on each piece, using nine different decal designs. Each piece is shaded blue on top to brown on the bottom with a gold rim on the edges. Serving pieces are more perfectly molded than the plates, cups, and saucers. Only the teapot includes the Kewpie trademark that was manufactured in Germany. *Courtesy of June Nelson.* $800-1000.

    Teapot with cover 3" high,
    Creamer & covered sugar bowl,
    Six plates 2.5" diameter,
    Six cups & six saucers 2.25" diameter.

The Golliwogg character in books was illustrated by Florence Upton and written by her mother Bertha Upton between 1895 and 1909 (also see Golliwogg in the American section of *Playtime Pottery, Volume I*). Golliwogg stories included Dutch Wooden dolls. The red striped dress and the blue dress with stars were taken from the American flag. In another scene Golliwogg is shaking hands with a wooden soldier. These four pieces have English Register Numbers "R.E.G. 425168" dating them 1904. The porcelain is German, most likely made to order for an English Company. $300-400.

    Two plates 5" diameter,
    Tall cream pitcher,
    Little footed jug.

R.E.G.
425168.

"Gasoline Alley" is printed on the face of the pieces. It was a cartoon created by Frank King in 1918. The main characters were Skeezix, Uncle Walt, Rachel, Auntie Blossom, Corky, Judy, Doc, Uncle Avery, Bill, and Nina. The backstamp is "MADE IN GERMANY" in a circle, but does not give the manufacturer. *Courtesy of Flora Jane Steffen.* $300-400.

    Teapot with cover 3.25" high,
    Creamer,
    Two plates 3.12" diameter,
    One cup & saucer 2.75" diameter.

Another set from the same mold is "SMITTY" from a comic strip created by Walter Berndt in 1922. The characters include Smitty, Herby, Mr. Bailey, and the dog Scraps. The plate is 4.37 inches in diameter. $50-100.

This particular mold has appeared with a number of different decorations. These decals depict a well-dressed man and woman in several outdoor scenes either walking, talking, or sitting. It would date early twentieth century. The mold is quite simple with a loop finial. The pieces are cobalt blue with a medallion picture. It also came in maroon. Some sets have embossed beading around the medallion. $300-400.

    Teapot with cover 3.62" high,
    Creamer & covered sugar bowl,
    Four cups & four saucers 3.75" diameter.

"Holland" is the mark on the pieces of this tea set. It is a pattern name rather than a country. It is German porcelain from the same mold as the preceding set. The note that came with this set reads, "These were my play dishes way back when - about 1908 or 1910, Marguerite." The Dutch scenes include two boys smoking pipes by the sea; a mother and daughter with ships in the background; and a father handing a boy a fish. It is cobalt blue with shades of blue in the decoration. $300-400.

    Teapot with cover 3.62" high,
    Creamer & covered sugar bowl,   **Holland**
    A small bucket 2.5" high,
    Serving plate 5.62" diameter,
    Four cups & four saucers 3.75" diameter.

"Delftina" is the pattern name of Dutch children decorating this doll-sized tea set. It makes sense that Germany would decorate with Dutch scenes because the countries border each other. Each piece has a Dutch boy and girl holding hands, kissing, or apart on the saucers. The colors are shades of blue. $300-400.

    Teapot with cover 2.5" high,   **Delftina**
    Creamer & open sugar bowl,
    Six cups & six saucers 3.25" diameter.

Halloween is coming, and here is the perfect child's set to use for decoration. These are the only pieces available to picture. The sugar bowl and cup are designed to look like a decorated pumpkin. The sugar bowl cover finial is in the design of a leaf and stem. This novelty item is German porcelain which was part of a child's tea set. $200-400. Full set $1000-1400.

Sugar bowl 3.5" high,
One cup & one saucer 3.25" diameter.

The Life and Adventures of Robinson Crusoe was written by Daniel Defoe in 1719. It is based on the story of Alexander Selkirk, a Scottish sailor who joined Dampier's expedition to the South Seas in 1703. After a quarrel with his captain, he lived on the island of Juan Fernandez for fifty-two months before being picked up.

This tea set is porcelain, decorated with decals and gold edges. The decals include Robinson Crusoe chopping a dug out canoe; watching natives by a campfire; talking with another man; running; and with a bird, dog, and cat. Other decals include Grandfather talking to three children; a child standing by a ladder; man with an arrow in his body; goats; a tall sailing ship; and a sinking ship. *Courtesy of Flora Jane Steffen.* $1000-1400.

Teapot with cover 5" high,
Covered sugar bowl,
Cake plate 4.5" diameter,
Six plates 2.75" diameter,
Six cups & six saucers 2.87" diameter.

Redware is a term used for wares made of red earthenware or red stoneware. These doll-sized redware sets are unmarked but in a letter Mr. Milbourn said he had this set marked and that it is German. It is doll-size circa 1900. If you rub the plates together, they have a clay sound. The pieces are all heavily embossed with flowers and leaves over a stippled background. The finial is a flower. The two sets shown are colored orange and dark brown. Each set, $200-300.

Teapot with cover 2.75" high,
Creamer & covered sugar bowl,
Four cups & four saucers 3" diameter.

"S. & G." is impressed on each piece which stands for Stephan and Gerabing, dating from 1887 to 1910. Terracotta is an earthenware body made of reddish clay and lightly fired. There is fine embossing on the low round serving pieces, covers, and cups. The cups are handleless with bowl-shaped saucers. It all fits on a large matching tray. $300-400.

Teapot with cover 3" high,
Creamer & covered sugar bowl,
Four cups & four saucers 3.12" diameter,
Tray 13.5" diameter.

S & G

It is always a great feeling to find an old child's play set still in its original box. It verifies the number of pieces that originally came packaged together, circa 1900. If you were to give this set a name, it could be called Tug-of-War. Decals include a boy with a hobby-horse and a big dog pulling the leash; a little girl pulling her doll from a big goose who has a hold of the foot; a girl playing with a string and four cats; and a girl hanging onto the tail of a big dog. The large open sugar bowl and saucers do not have decals. $300-400.

Teapot with cover 4" high,
Creamer & open sugar bowl,
Four cups & four saucers 4.25" diameter.

Here is another example of a fine German porcelain set found in the original box. The large open sugar bowl is almost the size of an English waste bowl. The sugar was coarse and you would use much more of it than we do today with refined sweet sugar. The sugar often came in uneven chunks. The decals are small, with two to four on each piece. The decals include a frog with a crown; a blackbird with a crown; an old man with a cane; an angel with a lantern; an angel in a flower; an Oriental person with a hat on his head. Gold trim completes the decoration. Other decorations were used on this mold. $300-400.

Teapot with cover 4" high,
Creamer & open sugar bowl,
Four cups & four saucers 4.25" diameter.

"M E, Bavaria, 19" is the trademark on this tea set. Bavaria is an area in Germany. The style and quality of porcelain should date this set early twentieth century. The set is decorated with a border of children in different types of dress and play. This set came in its original box with place settings for two. It also came in boxes with four or six place settings. $300-400.

Teapot with cover 3.87" high,
Creamer & open sugar bowl,
Two cups & two saucers 4.25" diameter.

**ME
Bavaria
19**

"M E, Bavaria, 66" is the same trademark as the preceding set. The number 19 or 66 are probably mold or decoration identification numbers for the factory. Number 66 has an entirely different mold and decoration than number 19. This set is oblong with eight panels. The decal is a horse's head. The luster trim is purple and orange. $300-400.

Teapot with cover 3.75" high,
Creamer & open sugar bowl,
Two cups & two saucers 4.37" diameter.

**ME
Bavaria
66**

A German novelty tea set is in the shape of chickens. The teapot, creamer, and sugar bowl are whole chickens. The teapot spout is the chicken beak and the handles are the tail feathers. The top rim of the cups have yellow chicken feet marks around the top rim. The comb and rims are red. $300-400.

Teapot with cover 3.75" high,
Creamer & covered sugar bowl,
Five cups & five saucers 3.25" diameter.
saucers 3" diameter.

Portraits are the theme on this cobalt toy set circa 1890-1910. The set is not trademarked but is a fine quality set. There is relief decoration on the teapot, around the base of the spout, and on the handle. The relief decoration is carried out on the cream pitcher and sugar bowl, the covers, and on the serving plate. The color is deep cobalt with gold trim and rims. $400-600.

Teapot with cover 4.75" high,
Creamer & covered sugar bowl,
Two serving plates 4 1/8" diameter,
Two cups & two saucers 3" diameter.

"MADE IN GERMANY" is marked on the base of the teapot. On the back is "A Present From Scarborough." Scarborough is in England so it stands to reason that this set was made for export. It is cute with cobalt trim on the front of the piece but would have been a cheap souvenir set. There is relief molding around the diamond shape design on all pieces. Covers fit loosely and the shapes are uneven. $150-250.

Teapot with cover 3.87" high,
Creamer & covered sugar bowl,
Two cups & two

Germany made some very fine quality play dishes. This set is fine porcelain with evenly placed decals, fancy openwork handles with gold rims, and gold trim over the cobalt blue band. This is an in between size, but closer to doll dishes. The set was probably intended for a little girl and her larger doll to have a small tea party. $150-250.

    Teapot with cover 4.5" high,
    Creamer & covered sugar bowl,
    Two cups & two saucers 4" diameter.

This doll-sized German tea set is decorated with cobalt bands and gold stars. It was probably sold through catalog sales or from a dime store in the early twentieth century. $100-200.

    Teapot with cover 4.25" high,
    Cream pitcher
    Serving plate 4" diameter,
    Two cups & two saucers 3" diameter.

This is another doll-sized tea set typical of early 20th century. It is cute but not a quality set. The fronts are decorated with a repeat pattern in cobalt blue with gold rims, handles, and spouts. $100-200.

    Teapot with cover 4.62" high,
    Creamer & covered sugar bowl,
    Four cups & four saucers 2.75" diameter.

"Germany" is marked on this fine set of porcelain doll dishes. It is well crafted with lovely shapes and a smooth glaze. It has blue hand painted decorations and a gold line trim on all pieces. $100-200.

    Teapot with cover 3" high,
    Creamer & covered sugar bowl,
    Six plates 3.75" diameter,
    Six cups & six saucers 3.25" diameter.

Germany produced a number of small cheap sets of dishes that were sold through mail order and dime stores from about 1900 to 1914. Decorations are painted over the glaze and usually show wear. The porcelain is thick and crudely potted. These sets should be priced inexpensively. They range from small doll-size to child-size. $75-125.

Germany is the country of origin for this set dated 1914. This German crest was used from 1914 to 1918. It is doll-size with oak leaves and acorns decorating the back of the teapot and cups. $100-200.
 Teapot with cover 3.25" high,
 Cream pitcher,
 Two cups & two saucers 2.62" diameter.

The only reason for showing this doll-size set is because it contains a tea warmer, which is also called a veilleuse (pronounced Va use). The extra long base on the bottom of the teapot fits into the top of the warmer which would hold a candle or fuel to keep the tea warm. The orange and black trim and gold bands have been hand painted. $100-200.
 Teapot unit 5" high,
 Plate 3.25" diameter,
 Cup and saucer.

There are all sizes of sets with trays made for children's play, doll dishes and miniature sets for doll houses. Other terms are a cabaret set for a tea table. A term for tea for two is Tête-â-tête or tea for one is a solitaire service. The next three sets fall in this category.

This set is fine German porcelain colored soft light blue shaded to yellow. It would date early twentieth century. It includes a tray 8.25 by 9.25 inches. The teapot handle is molded across the top. $200-300.
  Teapot with cover 3.5" high,
  Creamer & open sugar bowl,
  One cup & one saucer 3.75" diameter.

This tête-à-tête set has a background color in light blue with hand painted pink roses and green leaves. With the recessed cover on the teapot it would date earlier than the other two sets, circa 1890. The matching tray is 7.25 by 8.5 inches. $200-300.
  Teapot with cover 3" high,
  Creamer & covered sugar bowl,
  Two cups & two saucers 3" diameter.

This German service with matching tray, circa 1890 to 1915, is colored in light green luster and gold trim. The molds were ornate with embossing on all pieces. The matching serving tray is 8.5 by 9.75." $200-300.
  Teapot with cover 4.5",
  Creamer & covered sugar bowl,
  Two cups & two saucers 4" diameter.

"The 102nd Anniversary of the House of Steiff. Prior to 1903, Richard Steiff, the nephew of Margarete Steiff, designed a range of Teddy Bears. These bears became commercially successful at the 1903 Leipzig Fair in Germany and Steiff sold 12,000 pieces that year. 974,000 pieces were sold by 1907, and the Teddy Bear became a legend."

    "TEDDY BEAR TEA PARTY SETS, consisting of four bears: a white, a dark brown, a beige, and a caramel bear, together with a miniature china tea set, are being reproduced by old-time artisans to the same exacting standards as the priceless originals. These bears conform as closely as possible to the historic model of 1903."

    These sets are in honor of the 102nd Anniversary of the house of Steiff. That would date this new set 1982. The tea set is small size, the plates are 1.5 inches in diameter. A limited edition of 10,000 sets was issued. This set has the certificate number 5181. They were made in West Germany. $200-300.

Coffee Sets

A tall pot usually denotes its use as a coffee pot rather than a tea pot, especially pots with a high placed spout. The spout was high so that when the coffee grounds settled they would not pour into the cups.

Some sets that are an in-between size could be called either tea or coffee sets. The spouts were about in the middle of the pot. Even the cup shapes were generic.

A majority of the following coffee sets would date from the 1890s to the First World War in 1914. Most of these mold blanks came with numerous different decals for decoration.

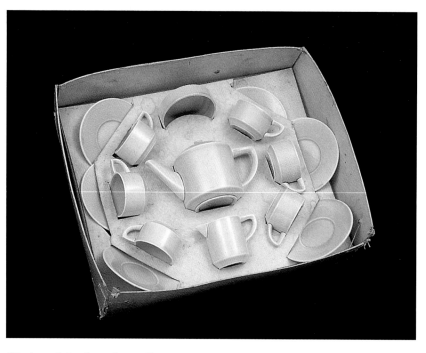

"Registered Geschutzt Depose'" is marked on each piece. It is from Waechterbach Earthenware Factory, Schlierbach, Germany. The company used this mark from 1894 to 1906. This earthenware coffee set came complete in the original box. It has a blue-gray glaze. The cups are in a low mug style. It is the type of set that would have been used in the kitchen or as a breakfast set. $300-400.

Coffee pot with cover 3.62" high,   Creamer & covered sugar bowl,
Six cups & six saucers 3.87" diameter.

Villeroy & Boch began a factory in 1836 when Eugene Francis Boch in Mettlach and Nicholas Villeroy in Wallerfangen, Germany became partners. Since that time and until 1931 they added factories at nine other locations in Germany. The V & B back-stamp is used in this chain of factories. V & B is the maker of the famous Mettlach steins. This is a nicely made tea or coffee service that is decorated in a pattern called "PAULA." The band and floral transfers are a deep blue-gray color. $600-800.

Serving pot with cover 5.75" high,
Creamer & covered sugar bowl,
Six plates 5" diameter,
Six cups & six saucers 4.5" diameter.

Villeroy and Boch in Wallerfangen, Germany, were the makers of this smaller tea or coffee set using the same trademark as the previous set. It is an in-between size, but closer to a large doll than a little girl. The set is earthenware with some crazing in the glaze. It has a graceful style. The decorative flowers, leaves, and border are blue-green monochrome transfers. $500-700.

    Coffee pot with cover 5.5" high,
    Creamer & covered sugar bowl,
    Four cups and four saucers 3.5" diameter.

Villeroy & Boch must have made quite a number of children's play dishes using this same mold, but with different decorations. "Made In Germany" printed on the mark dates it between 1935 and 1945.

The plate on the left is a stencil in rose and green. It is nicely applied under the glaze. The plate size is 5.12 inches in diameter. There is both a coffee set and a dinner set in this pattern.

The plate on the right is a brown monochrome with a fancy mark including the name "JARDINIERE." These sets are very similar in quality. The plate size is 4.75 inches in diameter. Each set $600-800.

Villeroy and Boch had a factory at Dresden, Germany, from 1856 to 1945. The china shown here is a white earthenware with blue underglazed transfer made at this factory between 1900 and 1910. This style server with the high spout is a coffee pot. The sugar bowl has raised lion heads on each side in place of handles. The blue underglaze design is a common pattern used by other potteries with some variations. The handles and finials are especially well designed. It is a quality set. This same pattern came in a tea set. The teapot shown matches the coffee service. It is 4 inches to the top of the handle. $600-800.

   Coffee pot with cover 6" high,
   Creamer & covered sugar bowl,
   Four cups & four saucers 4.5" diameter.

Villeroy and Boch also made this coffee set at the Dresden factory, using the same mold and trademark as the preceding set dating it 1900 to 1910. The light blue transfers are under the glaze. On one side of the server is a girl with angel wings holding a small tree, and on the other side a boy is carrying a shovel and a ball. Small objects are pictured in the other decorations. They include toys, such as a ball, top, and pull toys, or items found around the house such as a salt box, coffee grinder, funnel, spoon, scissors, needles and thread, books, horn, and violin. $600-800.

   Coffee pot with cover 6" high,
   Creamer & covered sugar bowl,
   Four cups and four saucers 4.5" diameter.

This German porcelain coffee service circa 1890 is exceptionally fine. The porcelain is thin with relief molding on all the pieces. It is embossed with scrolls and flowers with scalloped edges. The decals are like apple blossoms, colored from pink to red with shaded green leaves, giving the set a dainty, soft look. Edges are decorated with gold trim. $400-600.

Coffee pot with cover 6" high,
Creamer & covered sugar bowl,
Six plates 5.25" diameter,
Six cups & six saucers 4" diameter.

Another German porcelain set, circa 1890, is especially fine. It has embossed scrolling, extremely ornate handles, scalloped edges and graceful finials. The decals picture a little girl with a green dress, white apron, and a bow in her hair. She is holding up her apron, feeding the birds. $400-600.

Coffee pot with cover 5.75" high,
Creamer & covered sugar bowl,
Six cups & six saucers 4.25" diameter.

"MADE IN GERMANY" is marked on this coffee set circa 1900. The molds are especially nice with fancy embossing on all the pieces. The handles are unusual. Pink luster and a little gold trim compliment the set. The figures are of a Dutch boy and girl. Another scene pictures two Dutch girls and one boy talking. $500-700.

Coffee pot with cover 6" high,

Creamer & covered sugar bowl,

Six cups & six saucers 4.25" diameter.

This German porcelain coffee set features decals from Nursery Rhymes. It would date about 1900. The molds have embossing on all the pieces and the edges are scalloped. The added touches are the pink luster and a small amount of gold trim. The teapot pictures Snow White and The Seven Dwarfs. The plates have Red Riding Hood and the Wolf, Cinderella by the fireplace, and Hansel & Gretel by the gingerbread house. $500-700.

Coffee Pot with cover 6.5" high,

Tall creamer & covered sugar bowl,

Four plates 5" diameter,

Four cups & four saucers 4.25" diameter.

"G. H., GERMANY" marks this coffee set. The company is Gveiner & Herda that began in 1886. This mark was used in 1907. The molds have some embossing. There is extra gold trim designs on all pieces. The decal pictures a little girl and a boy with three large turkeys. $400-600.

    Coffee pot with cover 5.87" high,
    Creamer & covered sugar bowl,
    Six plates 5" diameter,
    Six cups & six saucers 4.25" diameter.

"MADE IN GERMANY" is the mark on this porcelain coffee service. It has embossed molding on all the pieces, trimmed in a light gray luster. The winter scene includes a horse pulling a loaded wagon; a horse pulling a sled; a front view of a horse pulling a sled; and a boy skiing. The colors are soft in brown, beige, and gray. $400-600.

    Coffee pot with cover 6.25" high,
    Covered sugar bowl,
    Three plates 5.25" diameter,
    Six cups & six saucers 4.25" diameter.

Teddy Bears were named after Teddy Roosevelt. In 1903 Teddy was on a bear hunt in Mississippi when he withdrew his gun on a charming little bear cub. The Ideal Toy Corporation of America asked permission to name their soft bear toys "Teddy's Bear's" which later just became Teddy Bears. Decals of bears were used on other toys. This nice porcelain coffee set with beading around each piece is decorated with a gold line trim. The decals include three scenes with teddy bears; two little girls with a teddy bear on a leash; a little girl washing her teddy bear; and a little girl standing in front of her teddy bear who is sitting on a stool. $600-800.

Coffee pot with cover 6.25" high,
Creamer & covered sugar bowl,
Four plates 5" diameter,
Four cups & four saucers 4.5" diameter.

This bear theme is from another German set with pink luster trim. The decal pictured has one adult bear teaching four small bears. The plate diameter is 5 inches. $50-75.

98

This German porcelain coffee set has especially appealing decals of children and toys. The two main decals are two girls and a boy playing ring-around-the-rosie. The second scene is of a boy standing by a big dog that has a basket handle in his mouth. On all the pieces there are extra toys and animals around the borders. $400-600.

    Coffee pot with cover 5.75" high,
    Creamer & covered sugar bowl,
    Six plates 5.25" diameter,
    Six cups & six saucers 4.25" diameter.

On fine porcelain, the bottom rim of the pieces is not glazed so the impurities may escape during firing. This set is better than average quality. It is manufactured of fine pure white porcelain with scrolling and scalloped edges. The theme of the decals are puppies and kittens. Gold trim decoration has been added. $400-600.

    Coffee pot with cover 5.75" diameter,
    Creamer & covered sugar bowl,
    Six plates 5.25" diameter,
    Six cups & six saucers 4" diameter.

German porcelain coffee sets are often unmarked, this one has decals of girls in dresses with long full skirts just standing or sitting around. The Victorian girls are all wearing hats. An embossed molding appears on all the pieces. There is no gold or luster trim, just decals for decoration. $400-600.

    Coffee pot with cover 5.75" high,
    Creamer & covered sugar bowl,
    Four plates 5.25" diameter,
    Four cups & four saucers 4.5" diameter.

This German porcelain coffee set has decals in soft colors. They picture three little girls sitting outside, under a tree, drinking tea. The main color is pink, with a little green and brown trim and a blue sky. $400-600.

    Coffee pot with cover 5.62" high,
    Creamer & covered sugar bowl,
    Six cups & six saucers 4.12" diameter.

An unidentified German factory produced the blank mold of this porcelain coffee service. It was decorated with numerous different decals. This particular set is decorated with a girl in a red dress doing different household chores. She is ironing on a board that is resting on two chairs, stirring a kettle on the stove, hand washing clothes in a tub, mopping the floor, feeding her doll, and carrying a market basket while holding an umbrella. $400-600.

    Coffee pot with cover 5.5" high,
    Creamer & covered sugar bowl,
    Six plates 5.25" diameter,
    Six cups & six saucers 4.75" diameter.

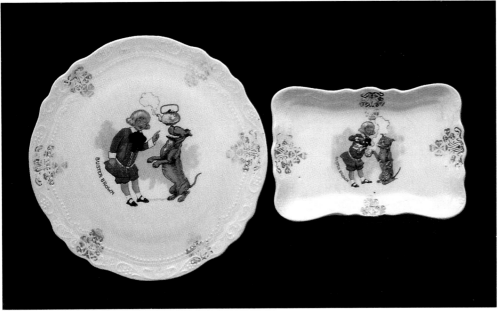

Buster Brown was created by Richard Felton Outcault (1863-1928). He began as a newspaper cartoonist and in 1902 created the characters Buster Brown, his sister Mary Jane, and Tige the bulldog. Buster Brown always had a prank to play, but the pranks were never mean, and always concluded with a useful little sermon for the children. This fine German porcelain set dates circa 1905. The coffee pot is delicate and it is a marvel that it has been preserved in mint condition. The two extra Buster Brown pieces are a hot pad 6.5 inches in diameter and a pin tray 3.5 by 5.5 inches. $1000-1400.

 Coffee pot with cover 5.25" high,
 Creamer & covered sugar bowl,
 Four plates 5" diameter,
 Four cups & four saucers 4.75" diameter.

GEE HOW YOU FRIGHTED ME

HERE TIGE

R. F. Outcault

R. F. OUTCAULT Buster Brown and Tige card of 1903.

Left:
"BUDDY TUCKER" is printed on the face of this plate. He is a character from the Buster Brown series written by Richard F. Outcault. The plate diameter is 5 inches. $35-65.

Below:
"MERRY CHRISTMAS" china tea or coffee sets are desirable to collectors of play dishes as well as to collectors of Christmas items. Most of these sets date in the early 1900s. This set has "MERRY CHRISTMAS" on each serving piece and cup. The other decoration is a Santa Claus dressed in a robe, carrying a Christmas tree over his shoulder, and talking with two children. A string of evergreens run across the top. The transfers are gold. The only color is the pink luster trim. $800-1000.

   Coffee pot with cover 4.75" high,
   Creamer & covered sugar bowl,
   Serving plate 6" diameter,
   Four cups & four saucers 4.5" diameter.

This Christmas scene includes an angel standing in a meadow. Pine trees and a building are in the background with a bright star shinning in a blue sky. The little bridge is over blue water. "MERRY CHRISTMAS" is written in black letters below the scene. The angel came in either a pink or blue gown. The set is produced in nice porcelain with embossed trim and fancy handles. Gold decoration completes the set. $1000-1400.

Coffee pot with cover 6" high,
Creamer & covered sugar bowl,
Four cups & four saucers 4.25" diameter.

Another version of the Christmas Angel has a darker background. "MERRY CHRISTMAS" is printed below the picture on the coffee pot but not on the other pieces. The design on the decal is the same. However, this set has darker pink on the angel, dark green trees, a darker colored house and bridge. It is porcelain with a little gold trim on a smaller blank than the previous set. It would date early 1900s. $600-800.

Coffee pot with cover 5.5" high,
Creamer & covered sugar bowl,
Two cups & two saucers 4" diameter.

There is a series of angel decorated sets. These sets have an angel face with wings in the upper background. A church and pine trees are also in each background. Here are the descriptions of three patterns. There is probably a fourth design. The mug is referred to as "Mary and Joseph and the Donkey" but it is not an official name. A man carrying a Christmas tree is pointing to an inn. A lady with a halo is riding a donkey.
The second scene pictures a man riding one of two horses with a whip in his hand. The horses are pulling a chariot with an angel holding a Christmas tree. The plate is 6 inches in diameter. Each set $900-1200.

The third set in this series is a coffee service. It has a lady in a blue gown with a halo, pulling a sled filled with a Christmas tree, buildings are in the background. The caption "Merry Christmas" is written on the plate. $900-1200.

Coffee pot with cover 5.87" high,
Creamer & covered sugar bowl,
One serving plate 6" diameter,
Six cups & six saucers 4.5" diameter.

Santa Claus is dressed in a red robe, standing in a basket below a balloon or dirigible. The basket has dolls and toys hanging on it. In the second scene, the decal is Santa Claus standing in an early automobile circa 1910, handing toys to the children. The decals are bright with pink luster trim on all the pieces. This is a common blank mold also decorated with other decals. $1300-1700.

Coffee pot with cover 5.37" high, Creamer & covered sugar bowl,
Six plates 5.12" diameter, Six cups & six saucers 4.37" diameter.

"THREE CROWN CHINA, GERMANY" is the
trademark on the porcelain set. This colorful
winter scene includes a snowman surrounded by
four children. In another scene the snowman is
tipping his hat to the children. These are nice
bright decals with vivid colors in red, blue and
green. $600-800.
  Coffee pot with cover 5.75" high,
  Creamer & covered sugar bowl,
  Five cups & five saucers 4.25" diameter.

Another winter scene on this German
porcelain set pictures two children on their
sleds going down a hill. The boy is carrying a
Christmas tree and the girl has packages. In
another scene children are making a
snowman. $400-600.
  Coffee pot with cover 5" high,
  Large open sugar bowl,
  Four cups & four saucers 4.62" diameter.

"GERMANY" in a circle is the only mark on this
porcelain coffee service. Each plate has a different
decal with little decals around the borders. The
same decal figures are on the serving pieces.
$400-600.
An angel in a leaf chariot, pulled by a big bird,
A boy riding on the back of a grasshopper,
A witch with a cat and a large bird,
An elf figure pulling a small wagon,
An elf figure sitting on a mushroom facing a big
bird,
A boy walking with a large goose.
  Coffee pot with cover 6" high,
  Covered sugar bowl,
  Six plates 5.37" diameter,
  Six cups & six saucers 4.5" diameter.

105

This coffee service has been manufactured in fine white porcelain. The mold is quite plain and is decorated with decals and gold trim. The spout on the coffee pot is graceful. Each piece, except the saucers, has decals of two kittens. The saucers each have two small decals of animals such as kittens, chickens, a goose, a goat, a mouse, a pig, and a duck. $400-600.

Coffee pot with cover 6.5" tall,
Tall creamer & covered sugar bowl,
Four cups & four saucers 4.5" diameter.

"C. T., ALTWASSER" stands for C. Tielsch & Co., Altwasser, Germany. The trademark dates this set between 1909 and 1927. They began porcelain production in 1845. The back stamp shown is their latest mark and dates this set to around the turn of the twentieth century. This is one of the few German sets that includes the manufacturer's mark. The set is quite plain with mug-shaped coffee cups. The colorful decals picture children, dogs, chickens and toys. $400-600.

Coffee pot with cover 5.75" high,
Creamer & open sugar bowl,
Five cups & five saucers 5" diameter.

This coffee set is from a common shape mold. The decals are darling little children. It is wonderful to see a rag-a-muffin type dress rather than the fine clothes that children usually wore. One design shows a little girl with layers of clothes and a cap, holding a doll by the arm, with a white cat in the background. Another scene is of a little girl in a long dress and wooden Dutch-type shoes with a doll sitting by her side. There are four decals with scenes of boys: with a sword, horn, gun, and a teddy bear; with a gun and dog; with a hobby horse, ball and book; and one snow-skiing. $400-600.

Coffee pot with cover 5.25" high,
Creamer & covered sugar bowl,
Five plates 5.5" diameter,
Five cups & five saucers 4.5" diameter.

"GERMANY" is printed on this porcelain coffee set. The date would be early twentieth century. The decals are cartoon children playing active games such as football, baseball or roller-skating. $400-600.

    Coffee pot with cover 6.25" high,
    Creamer & covered sugar bowl,
    Six plates 5.25" diameter,
    Six cups & six saucers 4.75" diameter.

GERMANY

This German porcelain coffee set would date circa 1900. The decals were designed from the Mother Goose nursery rhyme, *This Is The House That Jack Built* . Here is the last verse of that rhyme. $400-600.

> This is the horse and the hound and the horn,
> That belonged to the farmer sowing his corn,
> That kept the cock that crowed in the morn,
> That waked the priest all shaven and shorn,
> That married the man all tattered and torn,
> That kissed the maiden all forlorn,
> That milked the cow with the crumpled horn,
> That tossed the dog,
> That worried the cat,
> That killed the rat,
> That ate the malt,
> That lay in the house that Jack Built.

Coffee pot with cover 5.25" high,
Creamer & covered sugar bowl,
Six plates 6.25" diameter,
Six cups & six saucers 4.25" diameter.

This German porcelain set is made from a common mold that was decorated with numerous different decals. The captions are in German, which indicates that this set was not intended for export. The decals include;

A little girl playing the piano with another directing, "Der Erste Unterricht" or the first lesson.

A girl holding a steaming bowl ready to feed a goose, "Noch Zu Heiss" or still too hot.

Children falling in the snow, "Schnee schuh rennen" or snow shoe running.

Two boys riding horses, "Hart an ziel" or hard on goal or boundary.

Children riding in a cart "Fin Stolzes Gespain" or one proud couple or team. $400-600.

    Coffee pot with cover 5.5" high,
    Creamer & covered sugar bowl,
    Five plates 5.25" diameter,
    Five cups & five saucers 4" diameter.

This pattern mold is the same as the preceding set. The colors are quite unique. The background is shaded blue to look like the sky, while the bottom portion is shaded in tones of greens to browns to represent the ground. The decorations are decals of darling little children. Each design includes four children playing ring-around-the-rosie, playing music, washing clothes and just talking. $400-600.

    Coffee pot with cover 5.5" high,
    Creamer & covered sugar bowl,
    Four plates 5.25" diameter,
    Four cups & four saucers 4.25" diameter.

"GERMANY" is printed on the bases. It has the same common mold as numerous other sets, but the decals are especially interesting showing children sleeping and awake. The decals include a little girl just sitting up with the sun shining in her window; a girl slumped over a table with the sandman sprinkling sand to make her sleepy; and the little girl asleep in her bed, holding her doll. The fourth large decal features a boy and girl walking and carrying books. There are small decals around the borders on the plates and saucers. The sizes are the same as the preceding set. $400-600.

    Teapot with cover,
    creamer & covered sugar bowl,
    Six plates, five cups and saucers.

Another attractive set with the same pattern mold as the two preceding sets is decorated with decals of different breeds of chickens. They are European breeds. The sizes are the same as the two preceding sets. $400-600.

    Coffee pot with cover,
    creamer & covered sugar bowl,
    Six plates, six cups and saucers.

This small German coffee service has no special characteristics other than just being a nice quality, attractive, porcelain set. It is decorated with fancy gold trim and decals of little bouquets of flowers. Little handles are on the serving plate. $200-300.

    Coffee pot with cover 5.5" high,
    Creamer & covered sugar bowl,
    Two serving plates 4.25" diameter,
    Four cups & four saucers 3.75" diameter.

"LEUCHTENBURG, GERMANY" is the trademark for C. A. Lehmann & Son, Kahla, Germany. It would date 1910. The theme of the decals is young men playing soccer, a most popular sport in Europe. The trim on the porcelain pieces is pink luster. $400-600.

    Coffee pot with cover 5" high,
    Creamer & covered sugar bowl,
    Four cups & four saucers 4.5" diameter.

Germany produced some porcelain sets in lower grade with no trademark. The plates and saucers are all a little uneven. It is decorated in pink with blue flowers and green leaves, gold rims, and handles. This mold was used with several different decorations. The handles and finials represent branches or twigs. There is some relief molding on the serving pieces and covers. $200-300.

Teapot with cover 5.25" high, Creamer & covered sugar bowl,
Four plates 4.5" diameter, Four cups & four saucers 4.25" diameter.

Right:
"P. K. SILESIA" is the trademark for the Konigszelt Porcelain factory in Silesia, Germany. It would date between 1910 and 1927. It has a classic coffee pot shape, a plain mold with a high spout and loop handle. The decoration is a strawflower in underglaze blue. This is the only piece of the set available to picture, it is 4.5 inches high. $50-100.

"ROSENTHAL, SELB, BAVARIA" used this trademark in 1910. The Rosenthal factory produced fine porcelains. The little floral decals are evenly placed and the gold rims are applied with great skill. Some of the pieces include the pattern "MARIA." $200-300.

Coffee pot with cover 5.87" high,
Six cups & six saucers 4.12" diameter.

"RUDOLSTADT, MADE IN GERMANY" is the information on this trademark. It is from the Beyer & Bock factory in Volkestedt-Rudolstadt, Germany. The figures on the set have been called by several different names but it does not have an official one. The decorations include colorful creatures or stickmen and a blue band. It is a nice quality set. $400-600.

Coffee pot with cover 6" high, Creamer & covered sugar bowl,
Six plates 5.5" diameter, Six cups & six saucers 4.25" diameter.

Happifats was designed from drawings by Kate Jordan. In 1914, Borgfeldt registered these figures as a trademark in the United States and Germany. Bayer & Bock used either of these backstamps. These figures were popular at the time of the Kewpies, in the early twentieth century. An article on Happifats states that both Germany and Japan made tea sets. This set was made by Bayer & Bock from the same mold as the preceding set. It is decorated with decals of Happifats in action and strawberries on all the pieces. The rims on this set are dark blue but it also came with reddish-orange rims. "H" is on the sweater of the boy doll. $500-700.

Coffee pot with cover 6" high, Creamer & covered sugar bowl,
Four plates 5.5" diameter, Four cups & four saucers 4.25" diameter.

"P.S., A.G. SCHIRNDING, BAVARIA" is trademarked on this set dating it from 1925 to 1927. German manufacturers made some fine porcelain play dishes with detailed transfers and gold trim. The transfers show two little girls with a dog and toys; two girls and two boys playing a game; three girls and a boy holding hands in a circle game; two boys on a teeter-totter with two girls watching; a boy and girl swinging around and a little girl sitting with her doll watching. The molds are similar to the next set. $300-500.

Coffee pot with cover 5.5" high,

Creamer & covered sugar bowl,

Six cups & six saucers 4" diameter.

The porcelain factory Schirnding, Bavaria, used this trademark from 1925 to 1936. It is fine porcelain with silhouette decals of children and animals. Four different scenes decorate this set of play dishes. They are a girl in a short dress holding a ball and feeding two rabbits; a boy holding a horse-pull toy, feeding a dog that is standing on his hind legs; a girl standing with a frog on her head, holding a puppy and talking to a dog; a boy wearing knickers with a large bow at his neck, holding a hoop, watching a pig eat. $300-500.

Coffee pot with cover 5.5" high,
Creamer & covered sugar bowl,
Four plates 5" diameter,
Four cups & four saucers 4.5" diameter.

"SCHONWALD" is the trademark for Schonwald porcelain factory dating it after 1911. There are no records for the company after 1937. The coffee pot also has the gold number 01162 which would be the guilder's mark. The porcelain and the molds are quality wares. The silhouette decals are black with the little girls in colored dresses. $300-500.

Coffee pot with cover 5.75" high,
Creamer & covered sugar bowl,
Four cups & four saucers 3.87" diameter.

"SCHONWALD" Company used a red trademark between 1911 and 1930. The green trademark under the glaze dates this set 1930. The colorful decals are Sunbonnet Babies doing their chores such as washing, hanging clothes, sewing and mending, cooking, and having tea while reading a book or knitting. Gold rims complete the decorations. The mold and sizes are the same as the preceding set. $700-900.

    Coffee pot with cover,
    Creamer & covered sugar bowl,
    Six cups and saucers.

"Registered Geschutzt Depose" is on these German earthenware dishes. They were made by Waechtersbach after 1900. This coffee set is pictured in a German toy catalog of 1924 to 1926. The information given is "Elegant sets for children, for games or general use put up in best quality cartons." This mold was used for decorated sets in other colors as well as other transfers or decals. This earthenware coffee set is decorated with a blue square transfer design under the glaze. This set is separate but matches a dinner service set. $200-300.

    Coffee pot with cover 4.5" high,
    Creamer & open sugar bowl,
    Six cups & six saucers 3.87" diameter.

"WAECHTERSBACH" is trademarked on this coffee set, dating 1890 to 1900. This coffee service is plain pink, but this mold also came decorated with transfers or decals. It is earthenware of average quality. $150-250.

    Coffee pot with cover 4.25" high,
    Creamer & open sugar bowl,
    Five cups & five saucers 3.25" diameter.

The trademark "THOMAS, GERMANY" is a division of the Rosenthal China Corporation. The company began using this mark in 1957. Rosenthal has always produced a fine porcelain. This is a contemporary pattern with designs that look as if they were taken from a child's drawing of children, animals, houses, and trees. It is a smooth white quality porcelain with all the decorations in green, orange, and black. $150-250.

    Coffee pot with cover 4.25" high,
    Creamer and open sugar bowl,
    Two plates 4.75" diameter,
    Two cups & two saucers 4" diameter.

"THOMAS, GERMANY" is the same trademark as the preceding set. The coffee set is fine porcelain even though the shapes look like they could be plastic. They would date in the 1960s. Again they used decals that look as if they were drawn by children. The colors are red, green, and black. The sugar bowl cover has a cutout for the handle of a sugar spoon. $100-200.

    Coffee pot with cover 4.25" high,
    Creamer & covered sugar bowl,
    Four plates 6.5" diameter,
    Four cups & four saucers 4.37" diameter.

There is no trademark on this coffee service but there are impressed numbers 3351 that look like German marks. The set is poor quality, probably after 1950. It is most likely a mass produced item. The decals are black silhouette children with colorful Japanese lanterns. The line trim is green. $100-200.
   Coffee pot with cover 4.75" high,
   Creamer & covered sugar bowl,
   Five cups & five saucers 3.25" diameter.

Schramberger
Degerlein
Ges. Gesch.

"Schramberger, Degerlein, Ges. Gesch." is trademarked. This indicates the location, company, and that it is a registered mark. It is an earthenware set, circa 1930s, decorated with silhouette girls dressed in an orange dress. A green trim and cover complete the set. $100-200.
   Serving pot 5.5" high,
   Creamer & open sugar bowl,
   Two cups & two saucers 4.62" diameter.

This set was purchased new in 1981 for twenty dollars. The box has the information "China Toy Set / Porzellan Kinderservice" on it. An applied label gives the following information: "Made for Neiman-Marcus in German Democratic Republic." It is heavy porcelain. The decals are a heavy thick-type paint that is applied over the glaze. The characteristics that indicate a new set are a heavier, thicker porcelain; paint-type decals; and an overall poorer quality than an old set. Some flaws on this set include specks of clay that were not scraped off before glazing; the clay used in the sugar bowl is more creamy than the rest of the set; and the glaze has not been evenly applied to the outside bottom of the pieces. The saucers are nice but are a thicker porcelain than the old saucers. The individual pieces are not marked. $50-100.
   Coffee pot with cover 6.5" high,
   Creamer & covered sugar bowl,
   Four cups & four saucers 4.5" diameter.

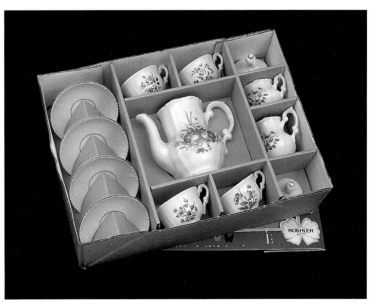

New porcelain sets are still being produced in Germany. They are quite nice but not as thin or as fine a porcelain as sets from the turn of the century. This coffee pot is trademarked "ROEHLER Collection, Made In Germany" but there is no trademark on the rest of the pieces. The information on the box includes "Fine Porcelain, Frankonia Toys." The decals include two rabbits and flowers on the teapot with just floral patterns on the cream pitcher, sugar bowl, and cups. Dark blue bands complete the decoration. $50-100.
   Coffee pot with cover 6" high,
   Creamer & covered sugar bowl,
   Four cups & four saucers 4" diameter.

Chocolate Sets

Chocolate or cocoa is prepared according to the custom of the country. Cocoa is the roasted, husked, and ground seeds of the cocoa plant. Chocolate is a preparation of the seeds of cocoa, often sweetened and flavored. If hot water and chocolate were mixed in the kitchen and served in the cups, you could add cream and sugar at the table. European sets would come with a milk or cream pitcher and a sugar bowl. The American custom was to mix the chocolate, milk and sugar in the kitchen so that it was ready to drink, therefore you would not need a creamer or sugar bowl with a chocolate set. The chocolate pot spout comes off the top rim and the cups are usually tall and narrow.

Above right and right:
These chocolate pots are from children's toy sets circa 1880. The tall pots would have included a tall creamer 3.5 inches high and a large sugar bowl 4.25 inches high. They are unmarked. One scene includes a man standing and reading a note to a woman seated in a Victorian chair. The other scenes are three young ladies in long Victorian dresses and hats being served fruit. Both chocolate pots have gold trim with green luster trim at the base. The pots are 6.5 inches high. Each pot $50-100. Set $400-600.

The tallest pot is fine porcelain, beautifully crafted and decorated. The colors and gold trim are hand painted over the glaze. Pink decorates the top and the border on the cover. On the bottom of the base, a star-shaped bit of extra porcelain has been added for additional strength. The largest pot is 7.5 inches high.
The smaller white chocolate pot has embossed flowers and trim with a little gold trim. It is 5 inches high. Each $100-200.

116

Right:
This German set, circa 1880 - 1900, has a tall serving pot with a large cream pitcher and sugar bowl. This set includes porcelain that is fairly heavy with gold trim on the front of the pieces and plain white on back. The decals are figures of a man and a woman either standing and talking or sitting and holding hands. $400-600.

    Chocolate pot with cover 6.25" high,
    Creamer & covered sugar bowl,
    Two cups & two saucers 3.75" diameter.

Below:
Cocoa sets are harder to find than either tea or coffee sets. Sunbonnet Babies on fine porcelain with ornate handles and finials make this set especially attractive. Green trim on the handles and rims set off the cute sunbonnet decals. The settings include a boy holding an umbrella over a girl, and a boy and girl playing horse with a rope. Other scenes include one or two girls with a doll, and with a wheelbarrow. *Courtesy of Doris Diabo.* $600-800.

    Cocoa pot 6" high,
    Tall creamer & covered sugar bowl,
    Four cups & four saucers 3.75" diameter.

This small German porcelain set is decorated with embossing and gold trim painted over the glaze. It does show wear. It would date early twentieth century. $200-300.

    Chocolate pot with cover 5.25" high,
    Four plates 3.25" diameter,
    Four cups & four saucers 3" diameter.

Oscar Schlegelmilch is the maker of this small chocolate set. He was a nephew of Erdmann and Reinhold Schlegelmilch of R. S. Prussia fame. He began his company in 1892 and this set is trademarked with the Gold Crown. The factory was located in the Village of Langewiessen, Thuringia, Germany, dating between 1900 and 1930. This chocolate set is beautifully decorated with cobalt blue bands overlaid with gold trim. The gold trim is prominent on all the pieces on the white porcelain and around the figures. The decal figures are Victorian in a garden setting. A large tray, 9 by 13.25 inches, holds the service. $400-600.

    Chocolate pot with cover 5.75" high,
    Creamer & covered sugar bowl,
    Two cups & two saucers 4" diameter.

This small porcelain chocolate set is twentieth century. The shape of the serving pieces are oval. Color decorations are under the glaze and the gold design trim is over the glaze on the green band and rims. $200-300.

    Chocolate pot with cover 4" high,
    Creamer & covered sugar bowl,
    Four plates 4" diameter,
    Four cups & four saucers 3.62" diameter.

Dinner Service Sets

"1 Stuch, Tafel Service" is the German label on this wooden box. Children on the cover of the box are dressed in costumes from 1860 to 1863. The wooden box size is 8 inches square by 4 inches high. The dishes could be a little later than the picture, probably about 1870s. The white porcelain dinner set is doll-size. It is trimmed with dark blue bands. It was purchased in Germany and was not intended for export. *Courtesy of Helga Stuewer.* $400-600.

Tureen 3.37" high,
Nine plates 2.75" diameter,
Two plates 2.5" diameter,
Six miscellaneous serving pieces.

Miniature dishes were used in doll houses or in the doll kitchens. Some of the German kitchens are called Nuremberg kitchens due to the large number that came from this area. One standard for miniatures is one inch to the foot. This set is a little larger and would be a good size for a doll kitchen. The porcelain is fairly heavy, potting is rather crude. There is nice embossing on all the pieces. Gold trim is over some of the embossed flowers and on the rims. $100-200.

A tureen 1.75" high,
Four soup bowls 2.12" diameter,
Five misc. serving pieces.

This set was purchased as a complete German dinner service. Pink luster on German wares was popular in the late nineteenth century in both children's and adult dishes. The serving pot does not have a cutout in the lid for a ladle handle. The dinner set, circa 1870, is more brittle than later wares. $300-500.

A tureen 5" high,
Platter 4.25 by 5.5",
Six soup bowls 4.25" diameter,
Four misc. serving dishes.

Below:
Meissen is the true maker of this little plate. It may have come with a dinner service set or a tea set. This trademark would have been used between 1814 and 1860. The plate is not perfectly round. It is decorated in blue underglaze with a fine smooth glaze. The size is 2.62 inches in diameter. $50-100.

Above:
"Blue Onion Pattern" is a familiar pattern that was designed by Johann Haroldt about 1730 at the Meissen factory in Germany. Johann Haroldt introduced this pattern when underglazed blue was being developed. He used designs of Oriental patterns, along with his designs of the Tree of Life, the chrysanthemum, the pomegranate, and a stylized peach (mistaken for an onion). Wares made at the Meissen factory have the crossed swords mark. The Blue Onion pattern was copied by other European factories. In Denmark a version was called Copenhagen pattern or Danish. This porcelain set is well crafted, hand painted in underglazed blue, circa 1880. The finial on the tureen is in the style of a pine cone. $400-600.

Tureen with cover 4.5" high,
Platter 3.5 by 5.75 inches,
Open serving dish 4.5" diameter,
Serving plate 5.5" diameter,
Three plates 4.75" diameter,
Three soup bowls 4.75" diameter.

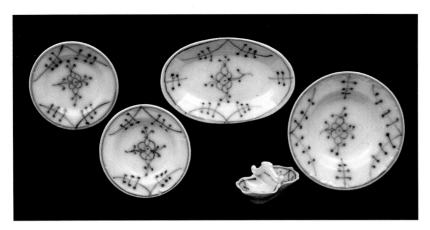

Meissen used a crossed sword mark and numerous other companies imitated and modified the mark. This mark is a variation of their mark but not made by Meissen. These particular marks are not listed in the German book of marks so the manufacturer will remain a mystery. This is a partial set decorated in underglaze blue. The center decoration is a straw-flower variation. A blue onion pattern is more valued than a strawflower. $100-200.

One platter 3 by 4.75 ",
Two bowls 4" diameter,
Two soup plates 3.12" diameter,
Two plates 3.12" diameter,
Small double dish.

Meissen trademarked these two pieces that complement the old pieces. They would date after 1921. Meissen is the State's Porcelain Manufactory in Saxony, Germany.

The egg cup and small covered dish with a flower finial are each 2.75 inches high. They are a nice size to add to a child's toy set.

The small oyster plate has a little different pattern but is similar in color. It has dips for five oysters. The plate is 4.37 inches in diameter. "S" in a shield is the impressed trademark for Bros. Simson, Gotha, Thuringia, Germany. The company mainly produced household china. Their wares would date 1887 to 1920s. Each piece $50-100.

Other German porcelain factories produced a wide range of quality toy dishes. This blue and white porcelain dinner set is a version of the Meissen blue onion pattern. The shapes are oval rather than the usual round tureen and covered serving dishes. $900-1200.

Tureen with cover, stand 4.62" high,
Two covered serving dishes,
Sauce boat, four-part divided dish,
Six plates 3.37" diameter,
Six plates 2.62" diameter.

Villeroy and Boch used this trademark at the Dresden, Germany factory between 1878 and 1930. This dinner service would date about 1900 to 1910. These pieces have been collected over a period of time and are in the same blue and white underglazed design as coffee and tea sets. There are twelve dinner plates to be used for two different dinner courses. One small oval serving dish has a basket weave on the outside. $700-900.

Covered tureen 4.75" high, Two platters 3.87 by 5.62",
Covered vegetable dish, Open serving dish, 5.37" diameter,
Two serving plates 5.12" diameter, Six soup plates 4" diameter,
Twelve dinner plates 4" diameter, Three small bowls, compote,
Mustard pot, two sauce pitchers.

Villeroy & Boch in Wallerfangen, Germany, were the makers of this child's dinner service set. The finial on the cover is a loop rather than a pointed shape. The cover does not have a cutout for the ladle handle. It is nicely decorated in blue monochrome border and floral design. Either trademark is used on this set. $700-900.

Covered tureen 6" high, Stand or underplate for tureen,

Two platters 5 by 6.25", Low footed compote 4.37" diameter,

Two open footed bowls 4" diameter, Ten soup bowls 4.37" diameter,

Nine plates 4.37" diameter.

"Villeroy and Boch, Wallerfangen" is the trademark on this set that is from the same mold as the preceding set. It also includes the name "Marchen." It would date 1900 to 1931. The green monochrome transfers include scenes from children's stories such as Red Riding Hood, Cinderella, a Prince, and animals. $300-500.

A tureen no cover 3.25" high,
Tureen stand,
Platter 5 by 6.25",
Serving plate 6" diameter,
Open serving bowl,
Sauce pitcher with attached underplate,
Four soup bowls 4.25" diameter,
Five dinner plates 4.25" diameter.

Dinner service sets are exciting to find because of the different shapes in every set. This fine porcelain set is not marked but has the quality of German wares circa 1880. The decorations are all hand painted under the glaze with gold trim over the glaze on the handles and finial. The outside border is light blue, the next ring is peach, and the large flower is purple. This is all connected with a wreath of stems and leaves. $400-600.

Covered tureen with underplate 5.75" high,
Platter 4 by 6.25",
One compote, sauce boat,
Covered serving dish,
Six plates 4.5" diameter,
Six soup bowls 4.5" diameter.

This set and the following set are not trademarked. They were purchased as French Limoges, but the characteristics and shapes fit the category of German, Bavaria, or Prussia more than French. The molds have embossing and the porcelain has a high ring when tapped together. The shape of the serving pieces, especially the pitcher, is a German shape rather than French. Both sets are a fine quality porcelain, beautifully molded and decorated with floral patterns and gold trim. This set has a background of one-half cream color and one-half peach color. The floral colors are yellow, orange and pink under glaze with gold trim stems and border lines over the glaze. $600-800.

Two covered serving dishes 3 by 4.25",
Small covered sauce tureen,
Two platters 3.25 by 4.25 ",
Open serving bowl, sauce pitcher,
Six soup plates 4.5" diameter,
Six plates 3.75" diameter.

This second set is white with a cream color border and gold trim. The center floral decoration has soft colors under the glaze. There is deep embossing on the molds especially on the corners of the covers and on the rims of the plates. $600-800.

Two covered serving dishes 3 by 4.25 inches,
Two platters 3.25 by 4.25 ",
One open serving bowl,
Six large plates 4.5" diameter,
Six small plates 3.75" diameter.

In the late 1800s Germany produced many fine children's play dishes. The set pictured is white porcelain with scrolling, decals of flowers, and a gold edge trim. This basic mold came with other decorations. $300-500.

Tureen with cover 3" high,
Platter 4 by 6 inches,
Two covered dishes 2.5" high,
Sauce boat,
Six plates 4.75" diameter.

"GERMANY" is the only marking on this fine white porcelain dinner set with embossed trim and beading on each piece. The theme of the decals is a circus. They feature a clown riding in a small cart being pulled by two pigs; a clown having dogs jump over a gate and through hoops; a monkey riding a horse; and an acrobat performing with two dogs. Other single decals are an elephant, horses, dogs, cats, clowns, and toys. This is a large-sized set on which little girls could actually have eaten their dinner. $700-900.

Tureen top size 3.75 by 5.75 ", Platter 5.87 by 9.75",
Large covered serving dish, Square open serving dish,
Four soup plates 6" diameter, Four dinner plates 6.25" diameter,
Four smaller plates 5.25" diameter, Four cups & four saucers 4" diameter.

Many unmarked porcelain sets are available in average quality but decorated attractively. The wide cobalt bands are under the glaze while the gold edging is over the glaze. It would be a perfect set to accompany a cobalt tea set. $200-300.

Large covered serving dish, 3 by 4",
Small sauce tureen 2 by 3",
Large platter 5.75 by 6.75",
Four dinner plates 4" diameter.

This German porcelain set is unmarked circa 1910. It is decorated with narrow cobalt bands under the glaze and gold trim over the glaze. It is interesting, but not a fine quality set. It would have been the quality from a cheap catalog sale or dime store. $100-200.

Tureen 3.25" high,
Platter 3 by 4.37",
Two open serving dishes,
Five soup plates 3" diameter.

125

Poultry is the theme on this dinner service picturing mostly chickens. The decals picture a girl feeding chickens on the platter. All the other pieces show one chicken or other poultry, featuring eight different breeds. $250-350.

Platter 2.75 by 4",
Serving dish 2.5 by 3",
Three soup plates & four plates all 3.25" diameter,
Five smaller plates 2.75" diameter.

"S & G" is the trademark for Schmelzer & Gericke from Althaldensleben, Germany. The company was in business between 1886 and 1931. This set would date between 1886 and 1910. This set is earthenware decorated with decals of two little children. The covers are decorated the same, but finials and designs are from different molds. $400-600.

Tureen with cover 4.75" high,
Platter 4 by 5.5",
Covered serving dish,
Open serving bowl,
Four soup plates 4.5" diameter,
Four plates 4.5" diameter.

Mildeneichen & Raspenau G. Robrecht began production in 1850 at Osterreich, Germany. This dinner set would date 1932. This earthenware dinner set is ivory colored, decorated with evenly placed decals of pinkish-red roses and green leaves. This is a large size for little girls to use. The set consists of twenty-seven pieces. $400-600.

Covered tureen 5" high,
Covered vegetable dish 4" high,
Platter 5.25 by 8.75",
Platter 4.25 by 7.25",
Two square dishes, sauce boat,
Six soup plates 6" diameter,
Six plates 6" diameter,
Six plates 4.75" diameter.

"WAECHTERSBACH" is trademarked on the sauce pitcher. It is from a dinner service set and would date between 1896 and 1910. It is decorated with four smaller decals from the story of "Little Red Riding Hood." The size is large for little children eating a meal with a base measuring 4 by 7 inches. $35-65.

"Registered Geschutzt Depose" is the trademark on this earthenware dinner set. The maker is Waechtersbach. It is pictured in a German catalog from 1924 to 1926. This set matches a coffee set but was purchased separately. It would be a nice size for a little girl's dinner. A washstand set also came with this decoration. $300-400.

Covered casserole with handles 5" diameter,

Covered casserole with handles 4.5" diameter,

Two open serving dishes,
Sauce boat,
Serving plate 7.25" diameter,
Four soup plates 5.87" diameter,
Four dinner plates 5.87" diameter,
Four small plates 4.62" diameter.

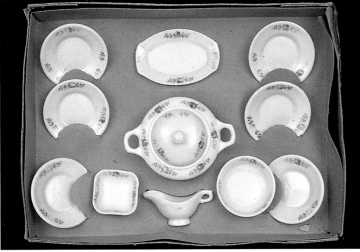

A small dinner set that came in its original box is earthenware. It is an inexpensive set that has been decorated over the glaze so it does show some wear. Dating would be in the early twentieth century. The large serving piece is a casserole dish or a soup tureen and the individual plates or soup plates are deep. $100-200.

Casserole dish 2.75" high,
Six deep plates 3" diameter,
Four misc. serving pieces.

Miscellaneous

A fish set is a rare find. This toy set is heavy porcelain circa 1880s. The fish and seaweed are molded in relief, then hand painted over the molding. The edges have a green luster trim. A set includes a platter for serving fish, six small individual plates, and it probably included a butter boat. $200-300.
   Platter 3.12 by 5 inches,
   Plates 3.37" diameter.

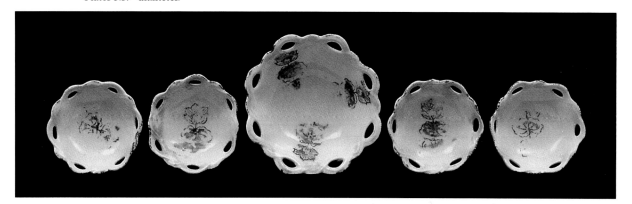

Germany produced numerous dishes, kitchen wares, dolls and toys, so every once in a while a different set surfaces. This set appears to be a nut dish set, circa 1910. It is German porcelain decorated with flowers and leaves, pink luster and gold trim over the glaze so there is some wear. The quality seems to be that of a toy. The large dish is three inches in diameter and the small dishes are two inches in diameter. There is no way to be sure of the intention of this little set, but it does resemble the large nut dish sets. It is always interesting to find new pieces and speculate on their use. $50-100.

"WAECHTERSBACH" is for the Wachtersbach Earthenware Factory located in Schlierbach. They used this trademark from 1896 to 1903. This factory made household and decorative earthenwares. Plates with cutout designs were strung with a colorful ribbon and hung for decoration. They are also referred to as ribbon plates. This plate is cream-colored earthenware, 3.87 inches in diameter. $75-150.

128

Above and right:
Novelty items were made for fun and may make you smile. This porcelain plate, 4.5 by 5 inches, is decorated with a decal of a little child sitting. On the back of the plate is the back of the picture showing the child on a potty. $35-65.

Ink stands are an interesting item for children. The holder with a wide hole is for the ink and the shaker holder is for the sand used to dry the ink. These heavy porcelain holders are perfect for a child's desk.
The white holder is 2.5 inches wide by 1.25 inches high.
The second holder is trimmed in green paint and gold trim. It is 2.75 inches wide by 2.12 inches high. Each $150-250.

Ink stands for children are copies of the adult sets. Another name is standish. This porcelain set has removable holders for the ink and sand and two holders for the quills or pens. It is decorated on all four sides with small hand painted flowers. It is embellished with gold trim. The back is 2.37 inches high, the base size at the feet is 2.25 by 4 inches. $200-300.

Wall pockets or hanging wall vases were made in toy size. They were intended to hang on the wall as a holder for flowers. They were decorated with a floral pattern or character figures, nursery rhymes, or animals. This mold has embossing and a floral decal for decoration. It is 4.5 inches high. $35-50.

German manufacturers produced small candlesticks in porcelain. The pair of tall candlesticks is 2.5 inches high. The cone shaped item is a candle snuffer. The short candlestick with encrusted flowers is trademarked Dresden. Each $50-100.

Chamber candlesticks have a handle and a saucer base to catch the wax drippings. The one on the left is trademarked "Dresden." The next three are samples of toy chamber candlesticks. The bases range from 2 to 3.25 inches in diameter. $50-100.

"GERMANY" is printed on the white chamber candlestick. It is molded to look like a basket weave, decorated with embossed flowers and leaves. A cheaper version are molded candle holders with "GERMANY 5096" impressed. The number is a mold identification. These are gold and blue luster with hastily painted flowers. They came in pairs. The bases are 3 inches in diameter. Each $10-25.

"Made In Germany" plus "K" in a circle are on the trademark. This pair of small vases (front and back) would date after 1891 and are more likely early twentieth century. They have applied flowers including a large rose, green leaves, and small flowers, called Elfinware. A little gold trim completes the decoration. They are inexpensive vases 3.37 inches high. Pair $15-25.

Below:
Jardinière is a French term for a large ornamental vessel to hold flowers. One jardinière is decorated in deep pink luster. It is a souvenir piece with "ATLANTIC CITY" printed on one side. It is 6 inches high with a 3.87 inch base. *Courtesy of Flora Jane Steffen.* The second jardinière is green to gray. The only other decoration is molding. It is 5.75 inches high. $75-125.

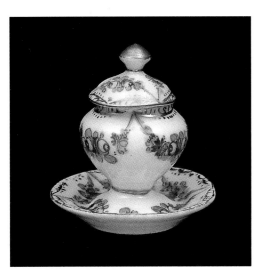

Left:
"H, X , Dresden" is trademarked on this covered piece. The German maker Franziska Hirsch used this mark until 1896 when Meissen contested the crossed staffs mark. This small covered jar is hand painted in the Meissen style with gold trim. It is 2.75 inches high. $35-65.

Wash Stand Sets

This German porcelain wash stand set in the original box is a great help in determining the number of pieces in a complete set. The red box is 11.25 by 15.25 inches. The background color is peach and the spongeware decoration is red. The brown branches, olive green leaves, and blue flowers have all been hand painted. Between the branches on the pitcher and wash bowl is one bird in flight. The complete set includes a wash bowl, water pitcher, soap dish, sponge dish with a cover, toothbrush holder with a cover, and a powder jar with a cover. This set does not include a potty. The mold and the sizes are the same as the next set showing different style of decorating. The date would be late nineteenth century to early twentieth century. This particular mold was produced in quantity with numerous decorating styles. $400-600.

This set is from the same mold as the preceding set. It is decorated with soft flowers on a blue-to-yellow background with gold trim. $400-600.

Water pitcher 5.75" high,
Wash bowl 7" diameter,
Toothbrush holder 1.5 by 2.5",
Soap dish 3.25" diameter,
Sponge dish 2.5" high,
Powder jar 2.75" high.

Wash stand sets in nice quality porcelain were produced by different manufacturers in Germany. This set is decorated with soft colored flowers and gold trim. This set includes a potty. $400-600.
    Water pitcher 5.5" high,
    Wash bowl 6" diameter,
    Covered soap dish,
    Covered toothbrush holder,
    Sponge dish,
    Potty.

Portraits of a lady make this an attractive set. This partial wash stand set is good quality porcelain. It is shaded blue in the background. $150-250.
    Water pitcher 6.5" high,
    Toothbrush holder 2 by 5.5",
    Potty.

Small potties were sold separately from the wash stand sets. Some were novelty items with captions such as: "GO WAY BACK AND SIT DOWN; MORNING EXERCISE; YOU NEVER HAD IT SO SOFT; MORE HASTE LESS SPEED;" and on one cover "DON'T LIFT THE LID." The large pots are approximately 1.75 inches high by 2.75 to 3 inches wide. The small pots with covers are about 1.75 to 2.5 inches high by 2 inches wide. Each $35-65.

A spittoon or cuspidor is round with a wide flaring rim. The small spittoons could have been used as individual pieces. The advantage of porcelain was that they were easy to clean. These two are 1.75 inches high by 2.5 inches wide. Each $35-65.

In Victorian times a lady always wore a hat, using hat pins to keep it on her head. When she came home and removed her hat she would place the hat pins in a holder. It would resemble vases or salt shakers with fewer holes, except they are solid on the bottom. The short holders are for stick pins and the tall holders for hat pins. This little hand painted holder has "Germany" printed on the bottom. It is 1.75 inches high. $50-100.

Bird-whistle cups were another novelty item for children. They are made of porcelain with a whistle in the shape of a bird that really works, circa1890-1910. One cup, 2.87 inches high, is hand painted. The second cup, 3 inches high, has a nice decal of two little girls and a dog looking at a parrot. Each $75-125.

Lithophane is a term for thin, translucent porcelain with a scene or design that shows when the light shines through. The mug and potty each have a lithophane in the bottom.

If a child drank all the milk from this special mug, a picture would appear on the bottom. It is 2.5 inches high. The scene is a child with a big dog.

The potty has a saying on the front, "Can you see through it," it is 2 inches high. The scene is a little boy ready to urinate. Each $75-125.

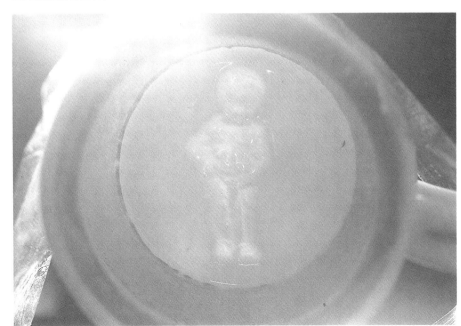

Italy produced ceramic wares since the sixteenth century. They were made of hard paste porcelain, soft-paste porcelain, and tin glaze earthenwares. There were factories all around the main cities plus smaller unfamiliar locations according to a map of Italian factories. The books talk about the type of wares made at these locations but there is no mention of children's dishes. There must have been toy sets made but since there were no export wares to the United States it is extremely difficult to identify what may have been made for children's play.

Italy

The Doccia factory near Florence was established in 1735. In 1896 Marchese Carlo II Ginori went into partnership with Jules Richard of Milan. The firm became Societa Ceramica Richard and Ginori. This tureen includes the trademark "Richard, Ginori, Italy." Another label reads "Finest In China since 1735." This small size tureen has a gold band and edge trim around an orange band. This twentieth piece is fine porcelain and I speculate that it may have come out of a set of children's play dishes. It is 3.5 inches high, the base is 3.25 by 5 inches. $50-75.

ITALY
106

Pink Poodle is the decoration on this earthenware tea set. It is reported to have been brought to the United States from Italy by a returning World War II serviceman for his daughter, which would date it in the 1940s. In addition to the usual tea service, other pieces include a bon-bon dish and a vase. The background color is pink, decorated with poodles, balls, and butterflies. It has vertical ribs and scalloped edges. The teapot spout is a dragon's head. *Courtesy of Clara & LeRoy Schiller.* $400-500.

    Teapot with cover 4.5" high,
    Creamer & covered sugar bowl,
    Bon-bon dish, vase 3.75" high,
    Four plates 6.5" diameter,
    Four cups & four saucers 5" diameter.

Japan

Dishes marked "Nippon" were produced for export only from approximately 1890 to 1921. Nippon is a name for Japan. Noritake china was produced by a factory in Nagoya, Japan, that was established in 1904 for the purpose of exporting. The wreath with an M in the center stands for Morimura Brothers who were New York importers. The green trademark was used for first grade wares and the blue trademark for second grade wares. In 1921 the word "Nippon" was changed to "Japan." In 1953 the center wreath was changed to an N for Noritake. In 1963 the name was changed to Noritake Co., Limited. Many items are hand painted and marked accordingly. Large quantities of Japanese play dishes were imported after the first World War in 1918 and before Japan's involvement in the second World War in 1941.

After the second World War some wares from Japan were marked "Occupied Japan," others were marked "Made in Japan" or just "Japan." America occupied Japan from September 9, 1945, to April 28, 1952. Japan continues to make china tea sets usually marked "Made In Japan" and exports them to the United States in quantity. This section should give a good sampling of the type of wares made for children's toys. Decorations are usually decals and the patterns are endless.

Factories that made tea sets for export quite often included dinner serving pieces to match. Some extra pieces may include a tureen, a platter, covered vegetable dishes, open vegetable dishes, a gravy boat, a cake plate, and salt and pepper shakers.

One feature that usually distinguishes a tea set made in Japan is the shape of the cup. It is a low round shape, with a plain loop handle. It comes small or large, fine quality porcelain to heavy porcelain, but usually of the same shape.

Japanese articles such as vases made in pairs were strictly for export. For their own use the Japanese made single pieces. Six plates or cups and saucers exactly alike were made for export. If it was for their home market it would have been a set of three or five with some slight variation in design or shape. The Japanese use small individual dishes rather than dinner plates. Large serving pieces and dinner plates were made just for export.

Japanese sets came with a basic unit of a teapot with cover, creamer and covered sugar bowl. This could include two, four, or six place settings. Larger sets often included a platter, covered serving dish, open serving dish, sauce boat, or cookie plate.

They vary in quality from fair to fine, but generally are of a mediocre quality. But remember, these sets were made as toys and were priced accordingly. They supplied catalog sales, dime stores or variety stores, department and toy stores. They were intended to be played with and, therefore, are easily distinguished from other fine china.

Japanese sets

This is a cadogan teapot. The example shown is from Japan. The design was taken from a Chinese peach-shaped wine pot. There is no cover, so it is filled through a cylinder from the base of the pot. The Staffordshire district potters made some of these pots but they turned out to be more of a novelty item because they were hard to clean. The background outline is a transfer with hand painted decoration over the transfer. The main enamel decorations are rose-colored flowers and green leaves. The butterflies, birds, and small flowers are multicolored. This cadogan pot is 3.25 inches tall. $400-600.

Celadon is a pale green or bluish-green tint glaze that imitates the Jade color. Chinese celadon appeared between 960 and 1279 and continued all through the ages. Jade was especially precious to the Chinese. Iron in the glaze gives the color its depth. Coal fuel produced darker colors than wares fired with wood. Celadon wares were produced in quantity between about 1820 to 1860. Celadon will vary in depth of color and thickness. Japanese celadons have a shiny glaze. This little celadon teapot is 2.25 inches to the top of the finial. It has a woven bamboo handle. Hand painted enamel decorations are green leaves next to white embossed flowers. $200-300.

"Satsuma" is the term used for a type of semi-porcelain. Korean potters settled at Satsuma, on the island of Kyushu, Japan, in the seventeenth century. Later, wares of this type but usually of inferior quality were made at Awata, Kyoto, Japan. These later wares were intended for trade to the European market. The term Satsuma usually indicates a cream-colored semi-porcelain with a finely crackled glaze. The decorations use enamel colors that have been hand painted. Decorations on this set includes birds, plants, and flowers in bright colors including raised enameling. There is no mark on this set which looks as if it would date about 1890. The handles and finials represent bamboo. $600-800.

Teapot with cover 3" high,
Creamer & covered sugar bowl,
Two cups & two saucers 3.25" diameter.

JAPAN

"JAPAN" is the only marking on this partial tea set. The early twentieth century pieces are a fine quality porcelain with a brittle feel and sound. Although there are no serving pieces for this set, it is included here because it is so unusual. The background outline is a transfer with all the color hand painted. The plates have two Oriental females walking down some steps by one person in a small boat. The cups and saucers show two figures. There are rocks, trees, and a building in the background. The enamel paint is heavy with raised enamel dots on the trees and in the border design. $200-300.

Four plates 5" diameter,
Four cups & four saucers 4.25" diameter.

JAPAN

"JAPAN" is the mark on this tea set. The quality is very similar to the preceding set. Serving pieces would probably be very similar also. The set has a transfer outline and hand painting over the transfers. It has bittersweet color edges and finial trim. The set is thin brittle porcelain. $200-300.

Teapot with cover 3.25" high,
Creamer & covered sugar bowl,
Two plates 4.25" diameter,
Two large cups & two saucers 4.5" diameter.

"JAPAN" is the mark on this tea set in the same series as the two preceding sets. It is incomplete but has interesting silhouettes of a little girl and animals. $200-300.

Teapot and cover 3.62" high,
Three saucers 4.25" diameter.

Above:
The Giesha Girl decoration has been a popular design on many play sets as well as adult sets. They were made in Japan and can be found in many sizes and variations in shapes and decorating. They were especially popular from about 1890 to 1930. These sets are usually a rather poor quality of grayish porcelain with flaws. They are a cheap copy of fine Japanese Kutani, made as export wares. This set has orange borders, handles, and a teapot spout that are crudely hand painted. The transfer background is a burnt orange color with some orange, yellow, blue, and green poorly applied. The sets were painted in typical oriental colors. The design includes two women and a child in a garden setting with Japanese lanterns overhead. $200-300.

   Teapot with cover 3.5" high, Creamer pitcher,
   Six plates 4.25" diameter, Six cups & six saucers 3.25" diameter.

Meissen developed the first porcelains in Germany in the 1700s. This pattern was used on tablewares and handles for eating utensils. Many wares with a blue underglaze are now referred to as Meissen Onion type, referring to the decoration rather than the company. This unmarked Meissen style set includes four little feet on each of the serving pieces and should date from about the 1880s to 1910. This set includes very thin porcelain, covers that fit loosely, and low round cups; features which give the feeling that it was made in Japan. *Courtesy of Flora Jane Steffen.* $300-500.

   Teapot with cover 3.5" high, Creamer & covered sugar bowl,
   Four cups & four saucers 4" diameter.

Left:
Japanese dishes of early 1900 were not always marked. The original box may have had "Made in Japan" printed on it. Decals on these plates and saucers are three poorly designed figures of a girl standing, a girl playing a violin, and a jester. It was difficult for the earlier Japanese artists to draw Western style people. It is decorated with a yellow band and gold rims. The base of the teapot is not glazed. $200-300.

   Teapot with cover 3.5" high, Creamer & covered sugar bowl,
   Four plates 4.75" diameter, Four cups & four saucers 4.25" diameter.

NIPPON

"NIPPON" is the only marking on this Japanese tea set. The sizes are very unusual. The teapot is small, the creamer matches the teapot, and the sugar bowl is large with a straight bottom, rather than rounded like the other pieces. The cups and saucers are large compared to the serving pieces. It is a fairly good porcelain with blue decorations. The scene appears to represent early America. There is a steamboat, trees, soldiers, oxen, horses pulling a covered wagon, men on horseback, and one man holding a flag. $200-300.

    Teapot with cover 3.5" high,
    Creamer & covered sugar bowl,
    Six cups & six saucers 4.5" diameter.

Above and right:

The Phoenix was a mythical bird that was consumed by fire and rose from the ashes after nine days to be young again. It is a symbol recognized in many countries. The Phoenix bird has dots on its breast. Phoenix variations for identification purposes include the names Double Phoenix, Flying Turkey, Flying Dragon, Blue Heron, Howo, Firebird, and Cobalt Bird. Phoenix Bird china was in production from the late 1880s until the 1940s with peak popularity in the 1920s. It was made for export. This transfer ware has at least 54 different backstamps mostly from Japan and a few known English pieces. This pattern was given as premiums as well as sold in stores. It is usually blue but the Flying Dragon and Flying Turkey may have come in green also. Included are different variations, sizes, shapes, and marks. This blue teapot, 3.75 inches high, cream pitcher and sugar bowl are marked with "M" in a wreath and "MADE IN JAPAN," circa 1915. The child's orange set is marked with Japanese Characters meaning Nippon or Japan. It was sent to the European market. The color is orange and is earlier than the blue pieces. The set came in the original box with a teapot and cover, four cups and four saucers. It didn't have a cream pitcher or sugar bowl. Each set $300-400.

    Teapot with cover 2.75" diameter,
    Four cups & four saucers 3.87" diameter.

This is an early twentieth century Christmas set. It has "MADE IN JAPAN" printed on the back stamp. The teapot has a Santa in a blue robe holding a bag of toys. The caption reads "Father Xmas Please send." The cream pitcher features a little girl talking on a telephone with the caption "Me A Doll." The sugar bowl pictures a boy standing talking on the telephone with the caption "Me A Gun." The four plates and saucers have the caption "Father X-Mas Please Send Me A Doll" or "Father X-Mas Please Send Me A Gun." $600-800.

Teapot with cover 3.5" high, Creamer & covered sugar bowl,
Four plates 4.25" diameter, Four cups & four saucers 3.5" diameter.

"MADE IN JAPAN" is the only mark on this tea set circa 1920s. It is a Japanese version of Sunbonnet Babies. The scene is taken from Bertha Corbett's book, *Here We Are At The Party*. The scene is similar, but the little girls do not have their dolls with them. It is colorful with gold trim on the edges, blue on the table cloth and green shading below the table. The girl on the left is dressed in a yellow dress and blue bonnet; the center girl has on a blue dress and pink bonnet; and the little girl on the right is dressed in a pink dress and blue bonnet. $600-800.

Teapot with cover 3.75" high, Creamer & covered sugar bowl,
Six plates 4.75" diameter, Six cups & six saucers 4.25" diameter.

MADE IN
JAPAN

This set has the rising sun trademark with the words "Hand Painted, Nippon." Dishes marked Nippon would date before September 1921. The pictures are black silhouettes. Black rims and yellow bands complete the decoration. The decals picture a girl rolling a hoop, a girl playing croquet, a boy and a squirrel, a rocking horse, and a girl on a swing. It is unusual to have five plates and seven saucers. Could it have been originally packed that way? They might have been short on plates in the packing house. They probably figured they would be played with and broken anyway. $300-400.

    Teapot with cover 3.75" high,
    Cream pitcher,
    Five plates 4.75" diameter,
    Six cups & seven saucers 4.5" diameter.

MADE IN JAPAN

"MADE IN JAPAN" is the mark on these dishes. There are numerous sets depicting the season or a simple outdoor scene. This set has a swan on the water with bushes or trees in the background. The colors are bright with a blue luster rim. They are hand painted so the colors vary on each piece. $200-300.

    Teapot with cover 3.25" high,
    Creamer & covered sugar bowl,
    Four plates 5" diameter,
    Four cups & four saucers 3.75" diameter.

"MADE IN JAPAN" in red letters is the only marking on this set. Japanese sets are more available today than sets from most other countries. Many sets are decorated with flowers and luster trim in mediocre quality. Some sets have more personal appeal than other sets. Special features on this set include blue birds, a soft blue border, line trim on all the pieces, and fine quality. The whole set is made of unusually thin, fine quality porcelain. $200-300.

    Teapot with cover 3.75" high,
    Creamer & covered sugar bowl,
    Six plates 4.25" diameter,
    Five cups & five saucers 3.75" diameter.

"NIPPON" is a word meaning "Japan." Dishes marked Nippon should be dated between 1891 and 1921 but there were always exceptions. This hand painted set is decorated with children. The figures are distorted, quite fat, with no necks and very little faces. The painting is colorful on very nice porcelain. This particular trademark is referred to as the rising sun trademark. $400-600.

    Teapot with cover 3.5" high,
    Creamer & covered sugar bowl,
    Six plates 4.5" diameter,
    Six cups & six saucers 3.75" diameter.

The Noritake trademark was registered in 1904 and used until 1941. This particular backstamp was registered in 1914. This set is produced using good quality porcelain. The decoration includes a soft green border with floral designs. The sizes and shapes are the same as the preceding set, but the quality is better and it includes the Noritake trademark. $600-800.

    Teapot with cover 3.5" high,
    Creamer & covered sugar bowl,
    Covered serving dish & platter 5 by 7",
    Four plates 4.25" diameter,
    Four cups & four saucers 3.75" diameter.

This "NORITAKE" set has the same mold and trademark as the preceding set. The "M" in the trademark stands for Morimura Brothers, who were New York importers. The mark also includes information that it is "HAND PAINTED" and was "MADE IN JAPAN." These wares are usually fine porcelain with lovely trim. This pure white set with gold trim has a very elegant appearance. It is a lovely set that could be mixed with decorations in a table setting. The added feature is the large matching cake plate. $600-800.

    Teapot with cover 3.75" high,
    Creamer & covered sugar bowl,
    Large cake plate 5" diameter,
    Covered serving dish & platter 5 by 7",
    Five plates 4.25" diameter,
    Five cups & five saucers 3.75" diameter.

This "NORITAKE" set is the third sample using the same trademark. The shapes are a little more rounded. It is a fine white porcelain beautifully crafted. The decorations are small flowers and a pink band with gold rims. *Courtesy of Isabelle Punchard*. $600-800.

    Teapot with cover 4.5" high, Creamer & covered sugar bowl,
    Large cake plate 5" diameter, Covered serving dish & platter 5 by 7",
    Six plates 4.25" diameter, Five cups & six saucers 3.75" diameter.

The fourth set with the same "NORITAKE" trademark uses another shape in fine porcelain. It is decorated from the story of Peter Pan. The hand painted colors of Peter Pan and Tinkerbell are red and pink with other accent colors. The story was written by James Matthew Barrie and opened as a play in London in 1904. The enchantment of the story is that children can fly and dreams really do come true. *Courtesy of Flora Jane Steffen*. $600-800.

    Teapot with cover 3.25" high, Creamer & covered sugar bowl,
    Three plates 4.37" diameter, Three cups & three saucers 3.75" diameter.

"NORITAKE" was the maker of this child's set in the Azalea pattern, the fifth set with the same trademark. Printed below the wreath is the information that it is "Hand Painted." This set dates from around the 1920s to the 1930s. This is a small-sized set in nice white porcelain, decorated with pink and white azaleas, green leaves and gold trim. The Larkin Company of Buffalo, New York, gave the Japanese Noritake Azalea pattern china as premiums with their soaps and other products or the public could purchase them outright. Their soaps were sold through mail order catalogs. In the late 1800s they included a handkerchief with the toilet soap and a bath towel with the laundry soap. They continued to expand the array of premiums. After 1900 the Larkin Company began to manufacture perfumes and pharmaceuticals. Around 1905 they added coffee, tea, extracts, and bakery products followed by paints and varnishes, and then furniture. By 1909, 900 premiums were available. Pottery and china items were so popular as premiums that John D. Larkin established Buffalo Pottery. The wares were used as premiums or sold directly to the public. As manufacturing prices rose, the company imported cheaper china for its premiums including the Azalea pattern. Azalea pieces were advertised from 1917 to 1940. $600-800.

Teapot with cover 3.25" high,
Creamer & covered sugar bowl,
Four plates 4.25" diameter,
Four cups & four saucers 3.75" diameter.

The sixth "NORITAKE" set has the same trademark but is of a finer quality. This is a doll-size set, smaller than most of the previous sets. The set is a deep pink with black trim. It would be a lovely set to use in a large doll setting. *Courtesy of Diane Punchard.* $600-800.

Teapot with cover 3.25" high,
Creamer & covered sugar bowl,
Six plates 3.5" diameter,
Six cups & six saucers 2.75" diameter.

In 1953 the Noritake china company changed the center "M" for Morimura Brothers to "N" for Noritake.

"NIPPON" is the only mark on this set of dishes. This indicates the approximate time period from 1890 to 1921. The features seem to date this set early twentieth century. The set is completely decorated in a blue-green iridescent luster. The shapes are quite unique for Japanese wares. Serving pieces are bulbous and the cups are more like European shapes. The inside of the covers are long and fit down into the teapot and sugar bowl. Applied finials are a little more ornate than usual. The porcelain is very thin and fairly good quality. $200-300.

Teapot with cover 4.5" high,
Creamer & covered sugar bowl,
Four plates 4.5" diameter,
Four cups & four saucers 3.75" diameter.

Japan exported numerous sets of play dishes with only the mark "MADE IN JAPAN" printed on the wares. This set represents typical shapes and quality of wares sold from catalogs and variety stores. Flowers and blue luster were both used often. The quality of this set is fine with a delicate cup, made of thin porcelain. A majority of the Japanese sets have this same shape cup. $200-300.

Teapot with cover 3.5" high,
Creamer & covered sugar bowl,
Four plates 5" diameter,
Four cups & four saucers 4.5" diameter.

MADE IN
JAPAN

148

Above and right:
"MADE IN JAPAN" is the mark on these luster tea sets. The back stamp is another version of the Rising Sun mark. They are typical of inexpensive wares sold from the 1920s to the 1940s. The larger blue-green luster set may represent Cherry blossoms which is the national flower of Japan. The smaller set is caramel luster with green luster handles and bases. It is decorated with a floral design. Each set $100-200.

Teapot with cover 3.5" & 1.87" high,
Creamer & covered sugar bowl,
Larger four cups & four saucers 3.75" diameter,
Smaller three cups & three saucers 3.25" diameter.

"MADE IN JAPAN" is the only mark on the tea set. The box cover gives this information: "Copyrighted 1917 Morimura Bros., The Little Hostess Tea Set, Trade Mark Reg in U.S. Pat Off. Made in Japan. " The cover also gives; *The Rules Of Table Etiquette For "The Little Hostess."*
1 - *SEATING THE GUESTS* — The places can be designated by place cards or as arranged by the Hostess. After the guests are all seated the Hostess takes her seat.
2 - *SERVING (A)* — Ladies should always be served before Gentlemen.
3 - *SERVING (B)* — The plate or cup should be passed to the guest nearest the hostess to her right, who in turn passes it along until it reaches the one for whom it is intended.
4 - *USE OF UTENSILS* — The knife should be used for cutting only, and never to carry food to the mouth. Only the spoon or fork should be so used. Between the mouthfuls the utensils should be placed on the plate until ready to use again, and not kept in the hands continually.
5 - *USE OF FINGERS* — The fingers can be used in handling the bone of a bird, or for asparagus, radishes, celery or olives.
6 - *CONVERSATION* — The guest should never criticize the food nor praise it unless asked for an opinion by the Hostess.

7 - *CLEANLINESS* — Guests should always come to the table with hand and face clean, the hair in order and clothes tidy.
8 - *USE OF THE NAPKIN* — The napkin should be held on the lap and not tucked under the chin; when through, fold it and place it on the table.
9 - *LEAVING THE TABLE* — The Hostess gives the signal by rising first; all the guests then rise and carefully lift the chair back so they can leave without making a noise.
10 - *GENERAL RULE* — The main object of Etiquette is to avoid causing displeasure or annoyance to others. By carefully watching one soon learns to become a pleasing and welcome guest, and will always be included when the list of invitations are being made out for the next party.
The porcelain dishes are average mass produced quality decorated in caramel luster. Tea sets in the original boxes were usually not played with very often, if ever. $150-250.

Teapot with cover 3.25" high,
Creamer & covered sugar bowl,
Four plates 4.25" diameter,
Four cups & four saucers 3" diameter.

149

This is an unusual interesting set with no back stamp. It is a dinner service set. The colors are caramel luster with a stylized black design in the blue band. There are no cutouts in the lids for a ladle. This set would fit perfectly with the previous caramel luster tea set. $200-300.

    A large covered serving dish 3.5" high, A small covered serving dish 2.62" high,
Six soup bowls 3.75" diameter,
Small platter 3 by 4.75" diameter, One round & one square open serving dishes,
One sauce pitcher with attached underplate.

KADEIN
JAPAN

Grill plates come with some Japanese sets. A catalog description is to "permit serving of meat and two vegetables on one plate." These range in size from 4.25 to 5 inches in diameter. Each $25-35.

"MADE IN JAPAN" is the only mark on this tea set. The set is decorated with caramel luster, a flower border trim, and blue rims. The serving pieces have a hexagon shape. The cups and saucers are the standard shape in a very thin porcelain. However, the plates are divided in three sections and are very heavy. They are called grill plates. $200-300.

    Teapot with cover 4.25" high,
Creamer & covered sugar bowl,
Sauce boat,
Six plates 4.75" diameter,
Three cups & three saucers 4.25" diameter.

150

Another set in the same mold has caramel luster with floral decals. It is a set with four place settings but also includes a cake plate, platter, covered serving dish, and a sauce boat. The sizes are the same as the preceding set. $200-300.

MADE IN JAPAN

"MADE IN JAPAN" is the only marking on this tea set. It would date about 1940s. It is a deep rose color. The design on this earthenware set is an embossed stylized leaves pattern on all the pieces. $200-300.

    Teapot with cover 3.25" high,
    Creamer & covered sugar bowl,
    Serving platter 3.75 by 5 .5",
    Two plates 5" diameter,
    Three cups & three saucers 4" diameter.

Japanese doll dishes often came boxed in a set of three place settings, as is the set shown here, circa 1915. The box size is 7 by 8.75 inches. The faces are painted a flesh color with rosy cheeks, blue eyes, red lips, and blond hair. The handles, spouts and saucers are green. The covers are maroon. A little verse is printed on the box. $200-300.

    Teapot with cover 2.75" high,
    Creamer & covered sugar bowl,
    Three cups & three saucers 2" diameter.

Dolly Tea Set
Here's a tea set for your
dolly and for you
And greetings for you both
go with it, too.

This Japanese tea set is unmarked. It came from England, which has different laws concerning trademarks. It is decorated with small flowers and gray luster trim. The unusual feature is that it includes a veilleuse (pronounced Va use). A veilleuse is a hollow pedestal with a heat source (a godet) to keep tea warm. $200-300.

A veilleuse 4 by 5.25" high,
Teapot with cover 3.75" high,
Creamer & covered sugar bowl,
Four cups & four saucers 3.87" diameter.

Some Japanese sets have a trade-mark that looks like a large bird in flight. This mark appears in black, red or blue. It is decorated with a gray band and silver trim. The most interesting feature is the graceful style of the cup, not the usual standard style cup. $200-300.

Teapot with cover 4.5" high,
Creamer & covered sugar bowl,
Four plates 5" diameter,
Four cups & four saucers 4.75" diameter.

Moss Rose design is decorating this twentieth century Japanese tea set. It has the same trademark as the preceding set. The most interesting features of this set are the extra serving pieces, especially the salt and pepper shakers. Other porcelain pieces found decorated with the Moss Rose are an egg cup and a small basket with a handle. $250-350.

Teapot with cover 5" high,
Creamer & covered sugar bowl,
Covered serving dish,
Platter 4.25 by 7.25 ",
Cake plate 6.25" diameter,
Six plates 4.5" diameter,
Six cups & six saucers 4" diameter.

Blue Willow is the best known Japanese pattern found in children's play dishes. They have been made in a variety of shapes and sizes. These twentieth century sets have been made for many years and were often sold through catalog companies. They were packaged with or without extra serving pieces. They may have included a covered serving dish, platter, gravy boat, cake plate, or salt and pepper shakers.

MADE IN JAPAN

The pattern basically is the Mandarin's pagoda, willow tree, bridge, runaway lovers, the boat that took them to their island, and the doves they turned into. The legend of the plate is printed in *Playtime Kitchen Items and Table Accessories.* $300-500.

Teapot and cover 4" high, Creamer & covered sugar bowl,

Covered serving dish, sauce boat, Platter 4.25 by 6.75",

Six plates 4.25" diameter, Six cups & six saucers 3.75" diameter.

The reason for picturing this very common set is that it is typical of the shapes and kinds of pieces that are included in Japanese sets. The set is marked "MADE IN JAPAN." It has a border design with a floral decoration. $200-300.

Teapot with cover 4.5" high, Creamer & covered sugar bowl,

Covered serving dish, Cake plate & platter,

Six plates 5" diameter, Six cups & six saucers 4.5" diameter.

This porcelain toy tea set in the original box is called "Classic Blue Bird Design." It was made in Japan by Yamada Toshio, Shoten, and was sold by Sears Roebuck & Company circa 1940 or later. The cover includes the information "An Oriental inspired formal tea set she'll use proudly." The transfer design is in blue. There are two birds sitting on tree branches with leaves. The border is narrow and quite plain. $150-250.

Teapot with cover 4.25" high, Creamer & covered sugar bowl,

Six plates 3.75" diameter, Six cups & six saucers 3.5" diameter.

JAPAN

"MADE IN JAPAN" is marked on these pieces. The plate pictures a teddy bear dancing with a girl. The cup just has the girl and the saucer has a tree. The background is a transfer, and all the colors are hand painted over the glaze. The rims are caramel luster. This plate, cup, and saucer are part of a child's toy set depicting the Teddy Bear. The plate measures 3.75 inches in diameter. $15-25.

The three little pigs is the theme of this novelty tea set. "MADE IN JAPAN" is the only back stamp marking. Serving pieces are molded in relief in the shapes of little pigs dressed as people. The covers represent hats. The cups and saucers have three little pigs painted on them. $150-250.

    Teapot with cover 3.5" high,
    Creamer & covered sugar bowl,
    Two cups & two saucers 3.25" diameter.

Novelty sets are fun for a child. They are created for pleasure, not quality. This Japanese set is in the shape of cats. The teapot cover is in the shape of a cat's head, it twists into place and does not fall off while pouring tea. The sugar bowl is a sleeping cat with a mouse for the finial. The black trim is hand painted. $250-300.

    Teapot with cover 5.25" high,
    Creamer & covered sugar bowl,
    One cup & one saucer 3.25" diameter.

"MADE IN JAPAN" is stamped on the pieces of this novelty tea set. The set is complete because it came in the original box. It is a porcelain of fair quality. The three serving pieces have handles in the shape of a dog. A dog and windmill are the decals used for decoration. The color is pea green with a blue rim trim. $300-400.

    Teapot with cover 3.75" high,
    Creamer & covered sugar bowl,
    Two plates 5" diameter,
    Two cups & two saucers 4.25" diameter.

"MADE IN JAPAN" is stamped on this set. It is the same quality and type of novelty ware as the preceding set. This set has a camel theme. The teapot spout has the likeness of a camel's head. The decoration is a boy riding a camel in the desert with palm trees in the background. $250-300.

    Teapot with cover 3.75" high,
    Creamer & covered sugar bowl,
    One plate 5" diameter,
    Two saucers 4.25" diameter.

"LICENSED BY FAMOUS ARTISTS SYNDICATE, MADE IN JAPAN" is the information on the teapot. Little Orphan Annie is a comic strip character created by Harold Gray (1894-1968). Mr. Gray was working as a cartoonist for the New York Daily News in 1924, when he started the comic strip, Little Orphan Annie. The comic strips had suspense, romance, danger, and thrills and they became an indispensable part of daily papers across America. These Little Orphan Annie dishes have different decal scenes of Orphan Annie and her dog, Sandy. $600-800.

> Teapot with cover 3.75" high,
> Creamer & covered sugar bowl,
> Cake plate 4.5" diameter,
> Six plates 3.75" diameter,
> Six cups & six saucers 3.25" diameter.

LICENSED BY
FAMOUS·ARTISTS
SYNDIQATE
MADE IN JAPAN

The information on the teapot reads: "BETTY BOOP, Des & Corp. by, FLEISCHER STUDIOS, MADE IN JAPAN." Bett Boop was drawn as an animated cartoon by Max Fleischer for Fleischer Studios, circa 1932. Betty Boop represents a movie queen of the 1930s. The Betty Boop tea set has the same style and luster trim as the Mickey Mouse and Orphan Annie sets. The figures shown are Betty Boop, the animal character Bimbo, and the cameraman Koko. $300-400.

> Teapot with cover 3.75" high,
> Creamer & covered sugar bowl.

BETTY BOOP
DES. & COPP. by
FLEISCHER STUDIOS
MADE IN JAPAN

These children's play dishes with Disney's Mickey and Minnie Mouse characters have information on the base of the teapot: "MICKEY MOUSE, Corp. by.. WALT E. DISNEY, MADE IN JAPAN." They would date from the 1930s. Walter Ellias Disney (1901-1966), better known as Walt Disney, was the producer of animated cartoons and the creator of Mickey Mouse, Donald Duck, and many other characters. Mickey Mouse was introduced in the first sound cartoon, "Steamboat Willie," produced in 1928.

This set of Mickey and Minnie Mouse dishes is decorated with blue luster and six different decals. They include Mickey and Minnie in a boat; Mickey showing Minnie a rabbit held by its ears; Mickey watering flowers; Mickey holding a microphone; Mickey painting; and Mickey blowing a horn. $600-800.

Steamboat Willie (1928), by Walt Disney, the first sound cartoon and the film that introduced Mickey Mouse

Teapot with cover 3.5" high,
Creamer & covered sugar bowl,
Six plates 4.5" diameter,
Six cups & six saucers 3.75" diameter.

This is another Mickey Mouse tea set with the same decals. The shapes of the pieces are different and the color is caramel luster rather than blue. By 1936 the George Borgfeldt Corporation of New York was distributing china play dishes of Mickey Mouse. $600-800.

Teapot with cover 3.5" high,
Creamer & covered sugar bowl,
Six plates 3.87" diameter,
Six cups & six saucers 3.37" diameter.

The information on the teapot is, "DONALD DUCK Corp. by, WALT E. DISNEY, MADE IN JAPAN."
Donald Duck is a Walt Disney character that first appeared in 1934 in "The Wise Little Hen." This set is an early version because Donald Duck has a longer pointed bill which was redesigned later on. The decorations are decals with caramel luster borders. This set would date in the 1930s. $600-800.

    Teapot with cover 3.75" high,
    Creamer & covered sugar bowl,
    Two cups & two saucers 3.25" diameter.

DONALD DUCK
COPR. by
WALT E. DISNEY
MADE IN JAPAN

This Donald Duck set has the information "MADE IN OCCUPIED JAPAN, © W.D.P.." This set marked Occupied Japan would date between 1945 and 1952, most likely in the late 1940s. Each piece of the set includes a picture of Donald Duck with blue trim on the handles and a border line trim on all the pieces. $500-700.

    Teapot with cover 3.25" high,
    Creamer & covered sugar bowl,
    Four plates 3.75" diameter,
    Four cups & four saucers 3.37" diameter.

MADE IN
OCCUPIED JAPAN
©.W.D.P.

"© 1937, W. D. ENT., MADE IN JAPAN" is the information on the teapot. Walt Disney Enterprises was established as a separate corporation in December 1929. "Snow White and the Seven Dwarfs" was Walt Disney's first feature-length animated film produced in 1937. These china dishes include colorful decals of Snow White, Doc, Sneezy, Happy, Grumpy, Bashful, Sleepy, and Dopey. The edges are trimmed in blue. A similar set also came trimmed in orange with larger, thin porcelain cups and no cake plate. $600-800.

Teapot with cover 4.5" high,
Creamer & covered sugar bowl,
Cake plate 5.75" diameter,
Six plates 4.25" diameter,
Six cups & six saucers 3.25" diameter.

© 1937
W. D. ENT.
MADE IN JAPAN

This Snow White set has a different Walt Disney mark. "©WDP." Snow White's dress is similar to the movie version. Snow White is on the front of the teapot, Dopey is on the back, Doc is on the creamer, and Happy is on the sugar bowl. The four cups picture Sneezy, Grumpy, Bashful, and Sleepy. The head of Snow White and a head of each dwarf are shown on the saucers. $600-800.

Teapot with cover 4.75" high,
Creamer & covered sugar bowl,
Four cups & four saucers 3.62" diameter.

©WDP

"Snow White and the Seven Dwarfs" was produced as a movie by Walt Disney in 1937. This set was probably produced after the movie and before Japan's involvement in World War II in 1941. The trademark gives the following information: "MARX TOYS, MADE IN JAPAN, LOUIS MARX & CO., INC. © WALT DISNEY PRODUCTIONS." This set includes some nice pictures of Snow White, the Dwarfs, and her Prince. This same china mold was used with Donald Duck decorations. $600-800.

Teapot with cover 3.5" high,
Creamer & covered sugar bowl,
Six plates 4" diameter,
Six cups & six saucers 3.5" diameter.

Above and left:
These sets appear to be Japanese with the bamboo handle on the teapot. The larger set is bright purple, the smaller set is bright green, and it also came in bright yellow. A yellow plate is marked "Made In Japan." There is no trademark on the other dishes. The box would probably have been marked with the country of origin. *Courtesy of Evan Punchard.* Each set $25-50.

Teapot with cover 2.5" high, smaller set 2.25" high,
Creamer & covered sugar bowl,
One saucer 3.5" diameter, two cups & two saucers 2.62" diameter.

Dishes made in Occupied Japan date after the Japanese surrender during World War II in September 1945. The occupation lasted until April 1952. In this short period of time only the mark on the dishes changed. The quality of the porcelain and the type of decoration did not change. This tureen or covered serving dish and platter include gold trim and hand painted flowers on a blue border. The platter size is 4 by 5.25 inches. $25-50.

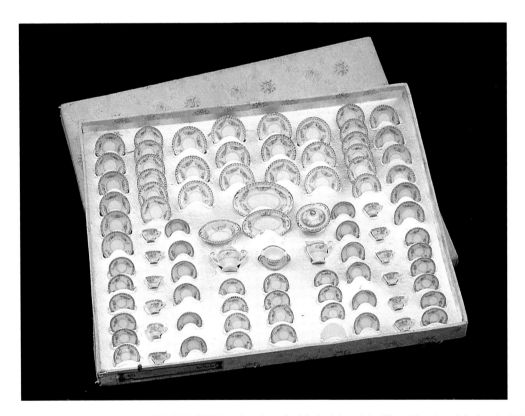

"MADE IN OCCUPIED JAPAN, TOY TEA SET" is printed on the label of the original box. The size of the box is 11.25 by 14 inches. The mark looks like it represents Mount Fuji. The date of this set is between 1945 and 1952. The set is small, the dinner plates are 1.5 inches in diameter. The pieces are porcelain but there is some variation in thickness and quality. Background floral designs are colorful transfers with hand painted trim around the outer border. A gold trim is on the edges, handles, and finials. The background is cream color with yellow trim and a white center. The whole set contains ninety-three pieces. $1500-2500.

Twelve dinner plates 1.5" diameter,
Twelve pastry plates 1.25" diameter,
Twelve cheese plates 1" diameter,
Twelve soup bowls,
Twelve salad bowls,
Twelve cups & saucers 1" diameter,
Large platter 1.5 by 2.25",
Smaller platter 1.25 by 2",
Covered serving dish,
Open serving dish, sauce boat,
Creamer & covered sugar bowl.

"MADE IN JAPAN" is marked on this coffee set. In a few cases, Japan produced some sets in a style not typical for that country. It is heavier porcelain and is a coffee set rather than the usual tea sets made in Japan, circa 1950. The cups are coffee mug shape. The leaf decals are blue, yellow, and pink with black accents. $75-100.

Coffee pot with cover 4.75" high,

Creamer & covered sugar bowl,

Six plates 4.5" diameter,

Six cups & six saucers 4" diameter.

"MADE IN JAPAN" is printed on the pieces. This style is typical of the 1950s. It is porcelain decorated with a large red rose decal. The rims all have a gold trim and gold handles are on the teapot, creamer, and coffee mugs. $75-100.

Serving pot with cover 4.75" high,

Creamer & covered sugar bowl,

Six plates 6.37" diameter,

Six cups & six saucers 4.37" diameter.

The printed mark is "MADE IN JAPAN." In the 1940s to 1950s it was popular to serve on a luncheon tray with a space for the cup. The size of the tray is 5 by 6 inches. It is decorated with yellow-gray luster, orange and purple flowers and green leaves. A set would include a teapot with lid, creamer, covered sugar bowl, with four cups and four tea trays. $75-100.

162

Indian or Native American portraits have been the subject on toy dishes. These twentieth century pieces are trademarked with a paper label "FAIRWAY, MADE IN JAPAN." The center portrait is an Indian Chief in a full headdress. The borders include symbols with English meanings. The category could be souvenir pieces. Germany produced sets with decals of Indians or embossed Indian faces. $25-75.

Teapot with cover 2.37" high,
Pitcher & one cup,
Plate & serving plate 4" diameter.

"JAPAN" is printed on the bottom of this tea set. It is doll-size purchased in the early 1960s. The box size is 5.25 by 7.25 inches. It has a dragon design in blue with a little gold gilding on each piece. It is a common Japanese practice to package sets for three, five, or seven place settings. *Courtesy of Diane Punchard.* $50-100.

Teapot with cover 2.25" high,
Creamer & covered sugar bowl,
Three cups & three saucers 2.25" diameter.

163

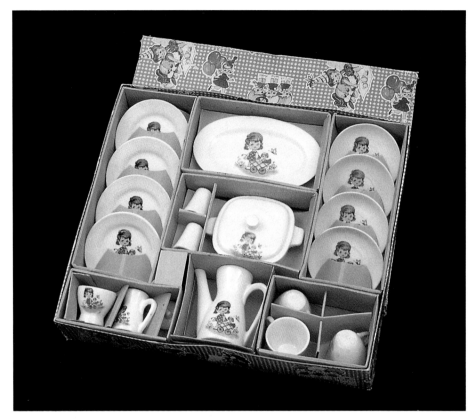

This Japanese set was sold in Switzerland in the early 1970s for 15 Swiss francs. The decals include a little girl standing by her doll carriage and doll. *Courtesy of Isabelle Punchard.* $100-150.

Teapot with cover 4.25" high,
Creamer & open sugar bowl,
Casserole dish, platter, salt & pepper shakers,
Four plates 3.87" diameter,
Four cups & four saucers 3.5" diameter.

This set on a tray was purchased in Japan in 1987. This would have been made for their home market. It is not marked because it was not intended for export. It is well crafted with a nice even glaze. The transfers are little children. $25-75.

Tray size is 3.5" by 10" long,
Teapot with cover 2.5" high,
Hot water pot,
One handleless cup.

Miscellaneous

"JAPAN" is printed on the base of this egg cup. It was used for a child rather than a toy. The height is two inches. It is decorated with a mother rabbit pushing two little bunnies in a small carriage. There are some sets of toy dishes that included an egg cup which is smaller than this one pictured. One is decorated with small red circles or large dots. $20-30.

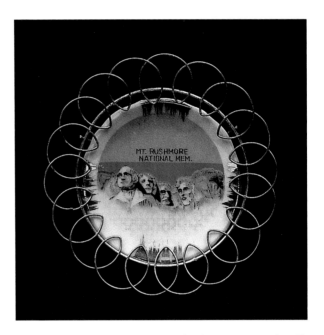

Cheap quality pieces are made in Japan for the souvenir market. They are often the size of toy dishes such as this little plate, 2.5 inches in diameter, in a metal holder. It advertises "MT. RUSHMORE NA-TIONAL MEM." This is typical of wares found at all tourist attractions. $5-10.

Dresser sets were toys to display on small dressers. "HAND PAINTED, M, NIPPON" is the information on this trademark. M is for Morimura Bros. importing Company. The porcelain pin tray matches two covered jars. The trim is green, yellow, and brown with gold bands. The tray size is 2.5 by 4.87 inches. The jars are 1.25 and 1.75 inches high. $150-250.

This child's dresser set has the blue Nippon rising sun trademark, dating early 1900s. It is porcelain decorated with hand painted flowers and trim. This set includes a hat pin holder 2 inches high, a hair receiver, and a hand ring tree. It should have a covered dish the same size as the hair receiver and a small round pin tray. $200-300.

Dresser sets came in all qualities. This is a crude porcelain set with poor painting. The original box reads "Made In Nippon." The pieces include a covered powder jar, covered hair receiver, ring tree, hat pin holder (2.25 inches high), and a cologne bottle. In this set a ewer has been substituted for the cologne bottle. $200-300.

"HAND PAINTED, OCCUPIED JAPAN" is on the trademark. Occupied Japan dates between September 9, 1945, and April 28, 1952. These three miniature pieces are extremely fine quality. They are made of thin porcelain, all three pieces include the same neoclassical designs surrounded in gold, plus heavy gold embellishment. The band trim is green, blue, and deep pink. Two pieces have matching handles. They were probably intended as curio cabinet pieces. The urns are 3.75 and 2.87 inches high. $200-300.

The Netherlands

The Netherlands is also called Holland or one could use the term Dutch wares. Delft pottery has been made in the Netherlands since the first half of the 17th century. In her book *European Porcelain* Marie Penkala documents eighty-two pottery factories that have operated here. Katherine Morrison McClinton writes "Miniatures were also made in blue and white Delft. There are single vases and complete mantle garnitures in Miniature size." Besides the Delft doll house or miniature pieces, were children's toy tea services made?

Petrus Regout founded the Maastricht "De Sphinx" factory. In 1836, he established a faience factory, and used printed transfer decorations in English style. Maastricht produced earthenware toy dishes in both tea services and dinner services. His son, Louis, was also involved with the company. "JOY, P. REGOUT" is the printed mark with an impressed oval trademark with the number 6 dating the set between 1855 and 1875. The earthenware is similar to English wares. The handles and spouts have a nice embossed molding. This mold shape is quite popular and was used often. The purple transfer includes a girl talking to a lady; three boys hunting, one with a bow and arrow pointing at ducks; three girls with a dog in a wheelbarrow; and two ladies with a dog. It has a wide intricate border. The cover was made on a wheel with the steam hole in the center of the finial. The deep color and interesting mold shape makes this an attractive tea set. $700-900.

Teapot with cover 3.75" high,

Creamer & covered sugar bowl,

Waste bowl,

Six cups and six saucers 4.25" diameter.

PETRUS REGOUT
6
MAESTRICHT

JOY
P. REGOUT

"P. Regout & Co., Maastricht" is printed in the Sphinx trademark dating it in the 1880s. The line below Maastricht is also used for dating. A break in the line under the letter M means 1883, under the A it means 1884, etc. A break in the line above P.REGOUT is also used for dating. A blank above the P means 1889, above the R it means 1890, etc.

The shape is the same as the preceding set but it was manufactured later with a well worn mold. The embossing is not sharp like the "Joy" set. It is decorated with dark blue transfers in a horse theme. The scenes include a man riding a horse past a building; a horse losing his rider; two people in a small cart being pulled by a horse; two people on a see-saw; and two men fencing. There are only three serving pieces, the same size as the preceding set. $300-500.

"SOCIETE CERAMIQUE, MAESTRICHT, MADE IN HOLLAND" is printed on the trademark. The spelling is Maestricht rather than Maastricht. This trademark was registered in 1900 and was used until 1940. It has the same shape mold but in a little larger size. It is decorated with decals featuring scenes of children with their toys and small animals. Pink luster trim finishes the decoration. $600-800.

Teapot with cover 3.5" high,
Creamer & covered sugar bowl,
Large waste bowl,
Four cups & four saucers 4.5" diameter.

The same trademark is used as in the preceding set. This set would date about the 1930s. The set has unusual shapes with a molded butterfly for the finials and handles on the sugar bowl. It is decorated with sheet pattern decals in small colorful flowers. From the collection of Kiok Siem. $600-800.

Teapot with cover 3.62" high,
Creamer & covered sugar bowl,
Four cups & four saucers 4.37" diameter.

The third set with the same trademark is still later. The earthenware is not as fine and it is decorated with decals and gold trim. There are chickens, ducks, and birds dressed in human clothes. These same decals have also been used on German china. $200-300.

Teapot with cover 4.5" high,
Creamer & covered sugar bowl.

169

The "MOSA" factory was established in 1883 at Maastricht. At its foundation it was called "Lewis Regout & Zonen." Lewis is the son of Petrus Regout. Now the name is "N.V. Porselein-en Tegelfabrick Mosa." They produce elegant table and tea services.

This Mosa coffee set is made of fine porcelain with an outside matte finish in an off white color, circa 1918. The coffee pot is in the shape of a cat with black ears and facial marks, with a red bow around his neck. The cream pitcher shows a duck with black tail feathers. The covered sugar bowl is in the shape of a rabbit with black on the ears, tail, and facial expression. They all have red eyes. Cups and saucers complete the set. From the collection of Kiok Siem. $700-900.

Coffee pot with cover 5.5" high,   Creamer & covered sugar bowl,
Four cups & four saucers 4.62" diameter.

This dinner service has impressed markings on different pieces which include "Wd., KN., K., & WR." These dishes are believed to have come from Holland circa 1800 to 1825, but this is open for discussion. The initials may be factory internal identification marks. This is a puzzle set as to the country of origin. It could also be German, French, or Scandinavian. The shapes and handles are so unusual that there are no pictures in my porcelain books to compare with these examples. The characteristics of this set include heavy hard paste porcelain. Extra stress porcelain has been added to the bottom of the larger serving pieces to give added strength. The blue band decoration has been applied over the glaze and does not show signs of wear. The gold trim has been applied over the glaze but years of wear and washing have worn off the gold in places. The shapes are particular interesting because they are so unique. All the handles are wing tip. The compote is made in two pieces and is held together with a brass bolt. The serving pieces have angled edges rather than round. This set includes forty five pieces. $2300-2700.

Soup tureen with cover 4.75" high, Two covered serving dishes 3.5" high,
Two small covered serving dishes 2.75" high, Compote 2.5 " high by 5.25" diameter,
Two pedestal open dishes, Double lip sauce dish,
Two double serving pieces, Platter 3.75 by 7.25",
Two platters 3.25 by 6.75", Two large serving plates 5.5" diameter,
Six small plates 3.25" diameter, Six soup plates 4.25" diameter,
Twelve dinner plates 4.25" diameter.

170

Creamware is light weight earthenware that was perfected by Josiah Wedgwood then copied by manufacturers in many countries. "P.R." is impressed for Petrus Regout at Maastricht dating this creamware dinner set about 1883. It is beautifully crafted with embossed molding on the finials and on the covers of the soup tureen and covered vegetable dishes. The whole compote is in the shape of a sunflower with leaves. The pickle dishes are all embossed. There are unusual pieces and unique shapes in this dinner set of forty-eight pieces. From the collection of Kiok Siem. $1300-1700.

    Soup tureen with cover 5.25" high, Two covered vegetable dishes,
    Two butter boats with attached bases, Three meat dishes,
    Small covered dish with attached base,   Two large serving plates,
    One serving plate with drain plate, Covered mustard pot with cover & ladle, salt & pepper spaces,
    One compote, two pickle dishes, Three open serving bowls,
    Eleven dinner plates 3.75" diameter, Six soup plates 3.75" diameter,
    Five small plates 3.25" diameter.

This set is from the same mold and has the same "P.R." impressed trademark as the preceding set. It is decorated with black transfers. Some horse scenes are the same as on the blue tea set. Other scenes include a girl jumping rope; a boy playing a drum; three children watching a puppet show; a boy on a rocking horse; soldiers by a tent; and children playing in a garden. From the collection of Kiok Siem. $1300-1700.

    Soup tureen with cover, One covered vegetable dish,
    Two butter or sauce boats, One large serving plate 5" diameter,
    Small covered dish with attached underplate, One pickle dish,
    Six plates & six soup plates all 3.75" diameter.

Petrus Regout of Maastricht fame produced Junior sets of dishes. Some pieces are potted thicker than others. "BORDURE" is the pattern name. The impressed cypher mark dates between 1890 and 1914. Under the pattern name in small letters is "9IIII" dating this set 1894. It has green transfer border designs. The size is in between a toy set and an adult set. Children could use this set for a complete dinner. There are a number of different patterns using this mold. From the collection of Kiok Siem. $800-1000.

Large covered tureen 6.5" high, Two covered serving dishes,
Large open bowl 7.5" top diameter, Two sauce boats, base 4.25 by 7.5",
Two compotes 6.25" diameter, Two condiment dishes 3.87 by 6.5",
Low pedestal plate 6" diameter, Two platters 5.25 by 7.75 & 5.37 by 8.25",
Twelve dinner plates 6.25" diameter, Twelve soup plates 6.25" diameter,
Twelve dessert plates 6" diameter.

BORDURE

Delftware is tin-glazed earthenware made at Delft, Holland, and also in England, which was introduced by Dutch potters. This little ceramic tray is a common type of ware that we associate as Delft in the twentieth century. Delft dishes of all kinds and tiles are a big industry from Holland. $35-65.

The tray is 4.5 inches in diameter with a .62 inch-high silver edge.

172

"Van Nelle" is printed on the face of the serving pieces and cups because this was intended for the Holland market. It did not have to be trademarked according to the United States requirements. This Blue Willow tea set is Japanese porcelain, but was made for Douwe Egberts Van Nelle Company between 1957 and 1964. Van Nelle is a factory for coffee and tea in the Netherlands. This is the first toy tea set that was offered from this company. From the collection of Kiok Siem. $200-300.

Teapot with cover 4.25" high,
Creamer & covered sugar bowl,
Four cups & four saucers 3.87" diameter.

This picture is included to show the different sizes from a junior set, an average toy tureen size and a doll sized covered casserole.

Norway

Norway is a long narrow mountainous country. On the other side of the mountains is Sweden. Most influences came from Denmark or from Britain across the North Sea. Norway was ruled by Sweden and in 1905 declared its independence. Norway continued its industrial expansion making pottery and porcelain for its home market.

Scandinavia - The four northern countries including Norway, Sweden, Denmark, and Finland have adopted the slogans: "Functionalism with Beauty," "More beautiful goods for every use," "Life is for living."

Scandinavian Nisse are imaginary creatures that live in every household. They're great little pranksters, but they are kind and helpful too. They see to it that the barnyard gates are closed, lost articles found, even that the milk doesn't sour. If the owners are good so is the Nisse. But if the owners are bad, the Nissen are busy causing trouble and being mischievous. The Nisse can peek out from around plants or furniture or any spot where he's comfortable. He can wake up and see who's around and what's happening.

Gnomes are little creatures that wear a high red-pointed hat. They keep an eye on the livestock as well as the crops and the household. Their stories are from Europe, Russia, and Siberia.

Nisse or Gnomes appear to be about the same little creatures.

Elves are an airy spirit with wings. They love dancing and playing instruments.

Goblins are dark little men dressed in black with small pointed caps. They are hateful, showing ill-will to others.

Trolls are from Scandinavia and Russia. Traditionally, they are stupid, distrustful, and ugly creatures.

Porsgrunds porselaen fabrik (porcelain) changed the spelling to Porsgrunn. The Porsgrund porcelain factory was established in 1887. In 1901, Rose Martin, the technical director at Porsgrund, introduced the technique of underglaze printing that had been perfected in Copenhagen. They produced artistic ware but after World War II they mainly produced quality hospital and restaurant wares. Scenic landscapes had a Norwegian flavor. Other patterns included Norwegian flowers and plants. The children's play dishes often included Nisse. This coffee set contains a oblong dish with cutout decorative sides, which would probably be considered a fruit bowl. The number 0280 on the teapot dates this set early 1890s. $600-800.

P P

Coffee pot 5.5" high,
Fruit bowl 4 by 6.5",
Three cups & three saucers 3.87" diameter.

Opposite page:
Egersund is a factory in Norway established in 1847. "Egersunds 7" is the impressed trademark. This Nisse pattern was used from 1892 to 1913. The transfer outline and border is brown with hand painted colors. The border is small and simple in design. The scenes include Nisse and children. Some small figures include a single child, a dog, chicks, holly, or a flower. This is a partial dinner service set but it also came in a tea service. The teapot shape would be almost identical to the teapots from Sweden or Finland. $700-900.

Large tureen 6" high,
Two large platters 5.87 by 8.12",
Open serving bowl 6" diameter,
Two plates 5.37" diameter.

EGERSUND

Poland

"S M, CHODZIES" is the trademark for Stanislaw Manczak in Poland. In 1920 the two companies merged. The factory is located at Kolmar in Posen, Poland. This trademark was used from 1928 to 1932. This earthenware soup plate came from a set of individual plates, and a platter and covered serving dish complete the set. It is a version of Snow White. The covered serving bowl is decorated with dwarfs around the center. Plate $20-25.

    Serving bowl 4" diameter,
    Platter 4" by 6.25",
    Six plates and soup bowls 4.25" diameter.

Portugal

Vista Alegre is a company that uses the initials "V A." The factory was established in 1824 by Jose Ferreira Pinto Basto. The factory is still in operation. Very little information is available on the types of work this company produces.

"VA, Made In Portugal" is printed on the base. It would stand for Vista Alegre Company. "Made In" on the trademark would date the set after 1891. The porcelain is white, decorated with hand painted flowers and leaves with ample gold trim. It is doll-size in the shape of French styles. $150-250.

   Teapot with cover 2.25" high,
   Creamer & covered sugar bowl,
   Two cups & two saucers 2" diameter.

"VA PORTUGAL" is printed on the base. Vista Alegre is the same company as the preceding set. This butter boat or sauce pitcher is a twentieth century piece. It is beautifully molded and decorated with a garland of gray flowers and leaves. Gold accents in the garland, on the handle, and around the base add a touch of elegance. The porcelain has a gray cast. If this piece is from a child's set, the whole set must be beautiful. The pitcher is 4.5 inches long by 3.25 inches high at the handle. $45-65.

"G. H. MAN & C., SACAVEMIN, MADE IN PORTUGAL" is printed on these twentieth century plates. They are 4.25 inches in diameter, which is child size, but there is no proof that any matching pieces exist. They are nicely decorated then glazed. One has colorful flowers and green leaves. The other one is brown with a white floral pattern. Each $20-25.

Russia

Kusnetzoff is the name of a family who owned and operated many porcelain factories in Russia throughout the nineteenth century and still remains in business. T.J. Kusnetzoff was the senior member who began a porcelain factory in Novocharitonowa in the early 1800s. It closed in 1870. In 1832 he opened a factory in Duljewo. After T.J. died, the business went to his son S.T. Kusnetzoff and in 1864 his grandson, M.S. Kusnetzoff, took over the family business. In 1842 M.S. opened a factory in Riga. In 1870 he acquired the Auerbach factory in Kusnezowo. In 1878 I.E. Kusnetzoff built the Wolchow factory. In 1887 M.S. founded the Budy porcelain factory near Charkow. In 1891 M.S. Kusnetzoff turned the family business into a company and absorbed many other small porcelain factories including the Gardner factory in Werbiliki. 1892 was the year for building a new factory in Slawjansk but it burned down in 1900. Also in 1900 I.E. Kusnetzoff took over the Merkur factory in Bronitzi and established a factory in Grusinow. During this time numerous different trademarks were used.

This small porcelain teapot has "MCKYZHEUOBA" printed in the trademark. It is from the porcelain factories owned by the Kusnetzoff family. It is hand painted with blue flowers, red accents, and gold trim. The teapot with cover is 3 inches high. $100-200.

The Gardner porcelain factory was established in 1754 by an Englishman, Frances Gardner, who had come to Moscow, Russia, eight years earlier. The factory produced tea and coffee sets and remained in the Gardner family until 1891 when it was sold to M.S. Kusnetzoff. This set was made by the Gardner factory during the reign of Alexander the III, dating it from 1881 to 1894. Russian porcelain can be heavy porcelain with bright colors, however, this set has a look of being cosmopolitan rather than Russian. This set is delicate in pastel blue with petite hand painted flowers and porcelain bows at the top of the handles. The quality is such that it could have belonged to an aristocratic family. $1000-1500.

N°6.

Teapot with cover 3.5" high,
Creamer & open sugar bowl,
Four cups & four saucers 4.25" diameter.

"Made in Russia by Kornilow Bros." is on the backstamp of these Russian pieces. Russian words are featured on the banner around the trademark. This set was made in St. Petersburg, Russia, before the revolution of 1917. Russian play dishes are rarely found in this country. The lid of the teapot has a steam hole in the center of the finial. The spout is unique with a fluted edge trimmed in gold. The hand painted scenes have a circus theme. The guilder's number 276 is painted on both pieces. The teapot pictures a large brown bear beating on a drum. The handle is a formed bear. The other decorations on the handle and spout are also hand painted. The trim around the lids and top of the serving pieces is a stylized design in green, brown, and gold. The sugar bowl has a large brown bear led by a person dressed in red carrying two flags, and a person dressed in red is walking behind the bear. Inside the handles is a molded brown bear. $300-400.

Teapot 3.75" high,
Covered sugar bowl 3.5" high.

Spain

The reference books talk about types of ceramics from the 16th to the 19th century that were made in Spain. There is no mention of any toy dishes although some were probably made in the late nineteenth century and into the twentieth century. From the map of factories from Spain and Portugal you would think that some play dishes were manufactured in this area, but it is difficult to find them in the United States.

Right:
"SPAIN" is printed under the glaze of this little plate. It is typical of the type of wares from Spain in the twentieth century. The colors are hand painted under the glaze. A bird is standing on a log. The main accent colors are green and yellow. The plate is 3.5 inches in diameter. $15-25.

Spain is producing new sets of dishes for children's play, such as this set from 1990. It is black with gold decoration. The shapes are uniquely different from other new sets. *Courtesy of Paula Gerdes.* $50-75.
   Teapot with cover 3.62" high,
   Creamer & covered sugar bowl,
   Two cups and two saucers 2.5" diameter.

Sweden

Sweden's economic strength began to improve in the late nineteenth century. By the early twentieth century industrialization created jobs and markets for their products. Ceramic designs usually reflected the home grown plants and motifs in simple repeat patterns.

Iron stone China
RÖRSTRAND

"Iron Stone Chine, RORSTRAND" is impressed on each piece. This mark would date this Swedish dinner service 1859. It has embossing on the finial and handles with green hand painting. The rims are caramel luster with an inside red accent line. $400-600.

    Tureen with cover 5" high,
    Serving bowl 5" diameter,
    Two platters 4.5 by 6",
    Five soup plates 4.62" diameter,
    Five dinner plates 4.62" diameter.

Rorstrand in Sweden established a pottery factory in 1726. There were different directors who brought their styles from Europe. Very good faience table services were produced. This impressed or printed trademark dates between 1884 and 1890. This earthenware set is decorated with blue transfer floral designs. It also came in black and possibly other colors. The mold is the same as a set from Finland but is not as fine a quality. This set does have crazing in the glaze. The platter, 4.37 by 6.75 inches, most likely came with a matching dinner service. $400-600.

    Coffee pot 5.87" diameter,
    Covered sugar bowl,
    Four cups & four saucers 4" diameter.

The same Rorstrand trademark is impressed on a few pieces. It is earthenware with some crazing. The outline for the floral design is a transfer with hand painted flowers. This is a matching dinner service set and a coffee set. The plates could be used with either the dinner or coffee service. The round tureen is unique with a well fitting underplate. Each set $400-600.

    Tureen with cover and stand 6" high, Coffee pot with cover 5.75" high,
    Covered vegetable dish, Creamer & covered sugar bowl,
    Sauce or butter boat, Six cups & six saucers 4" diameter.
    Two platters 4.37 by 6.75", Six soup plates 4.25" diameter,
    Six plates 4.25" diameter.

"PINOCCHIO, RORSTRAND, CO. WALT DISNEY" is printed on the pieces. Walt Disney produced Pinocchio as a movie which was released on February 7, 1940. Rorstrand in Sweden produced this coffee set called "Pinocchio." The decals include Jiminy Cricket, Figaro the cat, and Cleo the fish—but none of Pinocchio. It is earthenware from the 1940s with decals and hand painted black line trim with yellow bands and green accents on the teapot and creamer handle. In the story Geppetto was a kind old woodcarver that wished for a son, so he carved Pinocchio from a block of wood. Other characters in this story were Jiminy Cricket, Figaro the cat, and Cleo the goldfish. $400-600.

PINOCCHIO
Rorstrand
Ca.Wal Disney

    Coffeepot with cover 4.5" high,
    Creamer & open sugar bowl,
    Four cups & four saucers 4.25" diameter.

In 1878 Gustafsberg ceramics were featured at an international exhibit in Paris. The Gustafsberg factory was established in 1827 and is still in business. This earthenware set would date from about 1890 to the early twentieth century. It is smaller than sets from Rorstrand. The shapes, handles, and finial are all unique. It is decorated with purple transfers in floral patterns. $400-600.

    Teapot with cover 4.75" high,
    Creamer & open pedestal sugar bowl,
    Two plates 4" diameter,
    Two cups & two saucers 3.75" diameter.

"K P" are the initials for Karlskrona Porcelain located in Ussala, Sweden. This impressed trademark was used between 1918 and 1942. This child's set is larger than average. It is nice porcelain decorated with cute decals of children. The styles of clothes are from the 1930s. The children are with a doll, reading a book with a puppy by the girls' feet, playing with a doll carriage and holding a cat. $300-500.

    Teapot with cover 8" high,
    Creamer & covered sugar bowl,
    Two cups & two saucers 4.87" diameter.

"OPSALA, EKEBY, SWEDEN, KARLSKRONA" is printed on the trademark. The Karlskrona Porcelain Factory in Ussala, Sweden was established in 1918. This porcelain factory produces fine quality wares. The trademark on these pieces date from 1961 to the 1970s. The two cups are each decorated with decals of two children in an outdoor setting. The shape would be used for cocoa. They are 2.25 inches high. The cream pitcher and open bowl for sugar lumps, 2.62 inch diameter, are from another set. They are heavier porcelain but have the same trademark. Each piece $15-20.

Switzerland

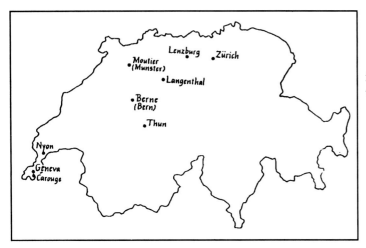

This map of Switzerland locates the ceramic centers. It is difficult to know what was made until dishes are found with trademarks.

Nyon, Switzerland, used the fish symbol to mark their wares. It was located on Lake Geneva from 1781 to 1813. After 1785 painter Jacques Maurer initialed his work J M. This is a lovely plate with cutouts in the border, hand painted flowers, and gold gilding. The size is 4.87 inches in diameter. $100-200.

"LANGENTHAL" is trademarked on this set from Berne, Switzerland. The company began production in 1906. They produced this fine porcelain set decorated with petite red roses, green leaves, and a gold edge trim. A child's set from Switzerland would more likely be for chocolate or cocoa rather than tea or coffee. See chocolate sets in the German section. The chocolate or cocoa was mixed with a little water and simmered. The milk jug is as large as the serving pot to be mixed in equal parts in the cup, then sugar was added. The cups are handleless. $400-600.

    Chocolate pot with cover 4" high,
    Milk jug & covered sugar bowl,
    Six cups & six saucers 3.5" diameter.

"Thoune" (pronounced "toon") is on the trade-mark. It is a chocolate set from Switzerland dating between 1920 and 1940. The pattern is "Edel-weiss," a classic Thoune design used in adult services as well as children's wares. It is decorated with a blue glaze with white raised flowers, leaves and trim. The body is pottery with a tin enamel glaze, similar to glazes on faience.
The story that came with this set was that a woman was served chocolate from this set as a child. She explained that there was no sugar bowl since the chocolate was already sweetened. The pitcher is a hot milk jug. Three cups are footed and smaller in size for the dark chocolate. The three larger cups were for milk chocolate, adding milk from the jug. $600-800.

    Chocolate pot with cover 6.5" high,
    Milk jug,
    Three smaller footed cups,
    Three larger cups,
    Six saucers 4.5" diameter.

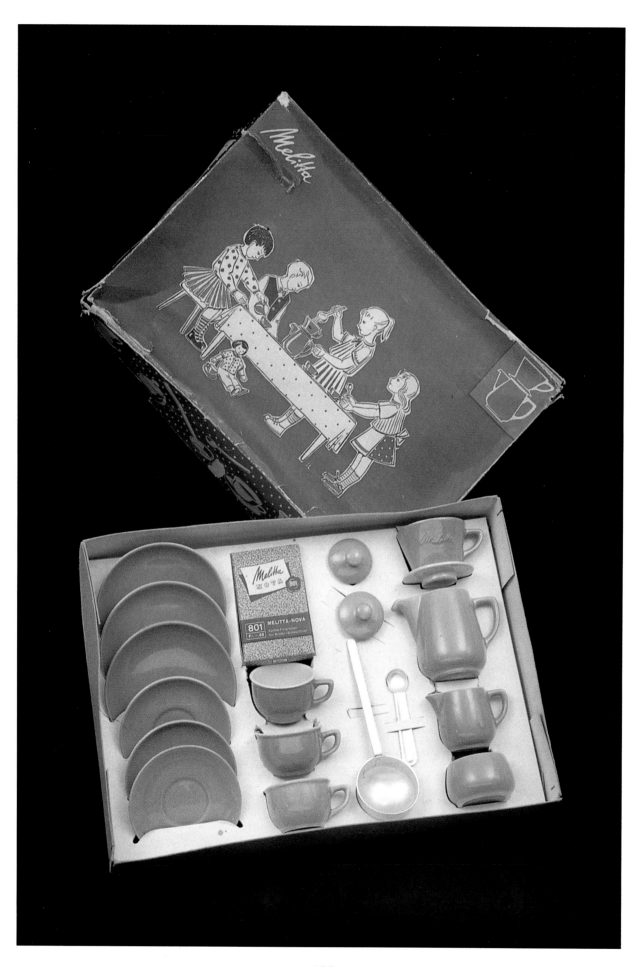

Opposite page:
"MELITTA, NOVA" is the maker of this pottery coffee set. The small box, 2.5 by 4 inches, which contains coffee filters has the information "Melitta, S.A. Zurich 9/48," dating this set September 1948. The cover of the box pictures children making coffee. The color is blue-gray. Included in the original packaging is a box of filters, an aluminum scoop and spoon, and a strainer for the coffee with three drain holes in the bottom. It is complete with three place settings. $100-150.

    Coffee pot with cover 3.87" high,
    Creamer & covered sugar bowl,
    Three plates 4.75" diameter,
    Three cups & three saucers 4" diameter.

"MELITTA, GERMANY" is printed on the base of the pottery coffee pot. It would date late 1940s. It is a different mold than the Melitta set from Switzerland. The top coffee strainer has one drain hole to drip into the coffee pot. The color is dark blue. $35-65.

    Coffee pot with cover 3.75" high,
    Coffee strainer, cream pitcher.

189

Bibliography

Bachmann, Dr. Manfred Commentary. German Toys Der Universal Spielwaren Katalog Hobby House Press, Inc., Cumberland, MD 1985

Barber, Edwin Atlee. Marks of American Potters Cracker Barrel Press, Southampton, L.I., New York

Brisco, Virginia - Everett, Shirley - Brisco, Bill. Torquay Mottowares Torquay Pottery Collectors' Society, Devon, England 1989

Coysh, A.W. and Henrywood, R.K. The Dictionary of Blue and White Printed Pottery 1780 - 1880 Antique Collectors' Club, Printed in England by Baron Publishing 1982 Volume II Antique Collectors' Club 1989

Coysh, A.W. Blue and White Transfer Ware 1780-1840 David & Charles, London 1979

Cushion, John. Pottery & Porcelain Tablewares William Morrow & Company, Inc. New York 1976

Cushion, John. An Illustrated Dictionary of Ceramics Van Nostrand Reinhold Co. New York 1976

Cushion, J.P. with Honey, W.B. Handbook of Pottery & Porcelain Marks Faber and Faber, London, Boston Fourth edition 1980

Danckert, Ludwig. Directory of European Porcelain N.A.G. Press Ltd, London (Published In English) 1981

Gaston, Mary Frank. Blue Willow Collector Books, Paducah, KY 1983

Godden, Geoffrey A. Encyclopaedia Of British Pottery and Porcelain Marks Bonanza Books, New York 1964

Godden, Geoffrey A. Encyclopaedia of British Porcelain Manufacturers Barrie & Jenkins, London 1988

Gorham, Hazel H. Japanese and Oriental Pottery Yamagata Printing Co., Ltd. Yokahama, Japan 1951

Greaser, Arlen e and Paul H. Homespun Ceramics Wallace-Homestead Book Co, Des Moines, IA 1973

Hake, Ted. Hake's Guide to Comic Character Collectibles Wallace-Homestead Book Co. Radnor, PA 1993

Hughes, Bernard. Victorian Pottery and Porcelain Spring Books, London 1959

Jackson, Mary L. If Dishes Could Talk Wallace-Homestead Book Co., Des Moines, IA 1971

Langham, Marion. Belleek Irish Porcelain Quiller Press Ltd, London 1993

Lehner, Lois. Lehner's Encyclopedia of U.S. Marks On Pottery, Porcelain & Clay Collectors Books: Paducah, KY, 1988

Lockett, T.A. Davenport Pottery and Porcelain 1794-1887 Charles E. Tuttle Inc. Rutland, VT 1972

Ludwig, Stefanie. Puppengeschirr Verlag Puppen & Spielzeug, Germany 1994

Marks, Mariann K. Majolica Pottery Collector Books, Paducah, KY 1983

McClinton, Katharine Morrison. Antiques In Miniature. Charles Scribner's Sons: New York, 1970

Milbourn, Maurice and Evelyn. Understanding Miniature British Pottery and Porcelain1730- Present Day Antique Collectors Club 1983

Miller, J. Jefferson II. English Yellow-Glazed Earthenware Smithsonian Institution Press, Washington, DC 1974

Miller, Philip and Berthoud, Michael. An Anthology of British Teapots Micawber Publications, Bridgnorth, Shropshire, England 1985

Penkala, Maria. European Porcelain Charles E. Tutle Co, Rutland, Vermont Second Edition 1968

Penkala, Maria. European Pottery Charles E. Tuttle Co., Rutland VT 1968

Punchard, Lorraine. Child's Play. Lorraine Punchard: Bloomington, MN, 1982

Punchard, Lorraine. Playtime Dishes. Wallace-Homestead Book: Des Moines, IA, 1978

Punchard, Lorraine. Playtime Kitchen Items And Table Accessories: Bloomington, MN, 1993

Riley, Noel. Gifts for Good Children. Richard Dennis, England 1991

Rinkker, Harry L. Warman's Antiques And Collectibles Price Guide, 28th Edition Wallace Homestead Book Co, Radnor, PA 1994

Rontgen, Robert E. Marks on German, Bohemian and Austrian Porcelain 1710 to the Present Schiffer Publishing Ltd. 1981

Salley, Virginia Sutton and George H. Royal Bayreuth China Portland Lithograph Co, Portland, ME 1969

Schneider, Mike. Majolica Schiffer Publishing Ltd., West Chester, PA 1990

Tardy. Les Poteries - Faiences Porcelaines, Europeennes Lengelle, Paris 1983

Tardy. Les Porcelaines Francaises, Paris, France 1987

Tijdstroom, De. Maastrichtse Ceramiek Uitgeversmaatschappij De Tijdstgroom Lochem / Gent 1985

Trimble, Alberta C. Modern Porcelain Bonanza Books, New York 1962

Van Patten, Joan F. The Collector's Encyclopedia of Nippon Porcelain Collector Books, Paducah, KY 1982

Van Patten, Joan. The Collector's Encyclopedia of Noritake Collector Books, Paducah KY 1984

Williams, Howard Y. Gaudy Welsh China Wallace-Homestead Book Co., Des Moines, IA 1978

Williams, Petra. Flow Blue China Fountain House East, Jeffersontown, KY Vol 1, 1971, Vol II 1973 Flow Blue China and Mulberry Ware 1975, Staffordshire 1978

Zuhlsdorff, Dieter. Marken Lexikon, Porzellan Und Keramik Report 1885-1935 Europa (Festland) Printed in Germany, 1988

Index